Country Editor
Henry Beetle Hough
and the Vineyard Gazette

Henry Beetle Hough at home in 1976.
Painting by Donald Carrick, courtesy of the Vineyard Gazette

Country Editor
Henry Beetle Hough and the Vineyard Gazette

Phyllis Méras

Phyllis J. Méras

Images from the Past
Bennington, Vermont

with the Martha's Vineyard Historical Society

Country Editor: Henry Beetle Hough and the *Vineyard Gazette*

Front cover and frontispiece: Oil portrait of Henry Beetle Hough by Donald Carrick, photograph by Ron Hall, courtesy of the *Vineyard Gazette.*

Upper front cover: Henry Beetle Hough at his desk in the *Gazette's* front office (detail), photograph by Gretchen Van Tassel, courtesy of the *Vineyard Gazette.*

Lower front cover and frontispiece: Cedar Tree Neck, Martha's Vineyard, photograph by Betsy Corsiglia from Corsiglia Fotografica.

Back cover: Henry and Betty Hough at a *Gazette* office window (detail), copyright Alfred Eisenstaedt.

Author photograph by Sal Laterra.

Library of Congress Cataloguing-in-Publication Data

Méras, Phyllis.

 Country Editor : Henry Beetle Hough and the Vineyard gazette/Phyllis Méras.
   p. cm.
 Includes index.
  1. Hough, Henry Beetle, 1896- 2. Authors, American–20th century–Biography. 3. Newspaper editors–Massachusetts–Martha's Vineyard–Biography. 4. Conservationists–Massachusetts–Martha's Vineyard–Biography. 5. Martha's Vineyard (Mass.)–Biography. 6. Vineyard gazette–History. I. Title.

 PS3515.O75933Z77 2006

 070.4'1092–dc22

                                    2006006221

 ISBN 1-884592-42-2 paperback

 ISBN 1-884592-45-7 hardcover

Copyright © 2006 Phyllis Méras

First edition
Published by Images from the Past, Inc.
www.imagesfromthepast.com
PO Box 137, Bennington VT 05201
Tordis Ilg Isselhardt, Publisher

with the Martha's Vineyard Historical Society
Edgartown, Massachusetts

Afterword by Richard W. Johnson
Executive Director, Sheriff's Meadow Foundation
Vineyard Haven, Massachusetts

Printed in the USA

Design and Production: Toelke Associates, Chatham NY

Printer: Thomson-Shore, Dexter MI

For
Bridie and Bonnie
and
in memory of Bunny

Martha's Vineyard

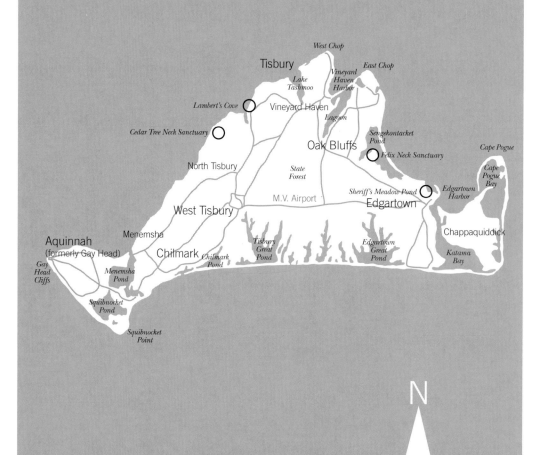

West Chop

Tisbury

Lake
Tashmoo

Vineyard
Haven
Harbor

East Chop

Lambert's Cove

Vineyard Haven

Cedar Tree Neck Sanctuary

Lagoon

North Tisbury

Oak Bluffs

Sengekontacket
Pond

Cape Pogue

Felix Neck Sanctuary

State
Forest

Cape
Pogue
Bay

M.V. Airport

Sheriff's Meadow Pond

Edgartown
Harbor

West Tisbury

Edgartown

Menemsha

Chappaquiddick

Aquinnah
(formerly Gay Head)

Chilmark

Chilmark
Pond

Tisbury
Great
Pond

Edgartown
Great
Pond

Katama
Bay

Gay
Head
Cliffs

Menemsha
Pond

Squibnocket
Pond

Squibnocket
Point

N

Contents

It is time to celebrate the life of this courageous country editor and to remember what he has meant to this island. I do it now when the Martha's Vineyard Henry Hough so loved seems to me to be in grave danger.

Today's Martha's Vineyard is far different from the quiet island—so green, so blue, so golden—to which Henry and Betty Hough came some nine decades ago. In summer, it bustles with tourists and bristles with television and political personalities. On waterfront promontories, the mega-houses of millionaires rise. Vineyard land values are among the highest in the nation. I fear for the island's future.

So I have finally written about Henry Hough, who had the perspicacity and selflessness to give precious land to conservation, who fought road-widening and black-topping, big buses, and the suburbanization of Martha's Vineyard.

This story of Henry Beetle Hough and the *Vineyard Gazette* is a tribute to a country journalist and to the influence of country journalism. Even in these times when television and the Internet rule the news, surely a place remains for such crusading country editors and for their newspapers.

Chapter 1

Pioneer Conservationist

The sun was blushing red above Nantucket Sound that late September day in 1976 when Henry Beetle Hough set out on his morning walk around Sheriff's Meadow Pond. His collie companion, Graham, bounding at his side, dashed off into the high-bush blueberry thicket every now and then, and returned to sneeze happily at his master.

For four-year-old Graham, the fifth in a series of Hough collies, it was like any other morning. First he had breakfasted heartily on a bowl of kibble and enjoyed a Milk-Bone treat. His master had finished another chapter of *Swann's Way* over his customary orange juice, shredded wheat, coffee, and toast before they set out around the pond. (Hough was surprised at himself that in his eighty years he had never read the Proust masterpiece. Now he was pleased that Vineyard summer visitor and Simmons College English professor Richard Freedman had urged it on him.)

Once man and dog were underway, there were, as usual, rabbits for Graham to chase and mallards to bark at. But for Graham's master, it was not an ordinary morning. Henry Hough had just learned that the Nantucket Sound Islands Trust Bill, designed to preserve the fragile Massachusetts coastal area of Nantucket, the Elizabeth Islands, and Martha's Vineyard, had died in Congress.

For more than half a century, conservationist Hough, in his weekly newspaper, the *Vineyard Gazette,* had been fighting to keep the woodlands and wetlands, the cliffs and dunes and moors of Martha's Vineyard as free as possible from overdevelopment.

On a clear September day fifty-seven years earlier, his bride-to-be, *New Bedford Evening Standard* reporter Elizabeth Bowie, glimpsing Martha's Vineyard for the first time, had exclaimed, "So sweet, so clean, filled with the bright hues of fall flowers and growing grass . . . so white, so blue, so green, so golden." And ever since, Henry Hough—and

Henry Beetle Hough and his faithful companion Graham on a stroll through Sheriff's Meadow Sanctuary. Established in 1959, the seventeen-acre sanctuary was the first of many conservation efforts on Martha's Vineyard initiated by Henry Hough and his wife, Elizabeth Bowie Hough. *Photograph by Edith G. Blake*

Elizabeth Bowie Hough until her death in 1965—had worked incessantly to keep Martha's Vineyard that way.

Rangy, bespectacled Henry Hough moved more slowly than usual that morning in 1976, for ordinarily he was a brisk walker. There were cones on the black alder he had planted in Sheriff's Meadow. The red and yellow bittersweet was out. Huckleberry leaves were turning red. He looked skyward as a flock of Canada geese swept overhead, wings whirring as they headed for an up-island field.

He and Betty had saved the woods and marsh where he was walking for future generations by establishing a conservation foundation in 1959 to protect them.

Although the Houghs' total joint income from the little newspaper they edited and published never exceeded $16,000, they had given the ten acres behind their house (valued at $40,000 at the time of their gift) to start the Sheriff's Meadow Foundation. And, with political skill, economic acumen, and determination that never waned (all of which seemed quite out of place in so seemingly shy a man) Henry Hough had persuaded his Edgartown neighbors to give away some of their land, too, to make Sheriff's Meadow a seventeen-acre wildlife preserve.

Pleased with his success with his Edgartown neighbors, the indefatigable conservationist-editor had then convinced landowners all across the Vineyard that they would be increasing their own land's value and helping retain the rural quality of the island, if they agreed to preserve some of their property as well. By 1976, he had done enough convincing so the Sheriff's Meadow Foundation had 770 acres that could never be built upon.

But he had hoped for much, much more when, in 1972, Senator Edward M. Kennedy had proposed the establishment of the Islands Trust. Such a trust, Ted Kennedy said, had been a dream of his brother President John F. Kennedy when he had started the Cape Cod National Seashore. Jack had envisioned saving the offshore islands in the same way that he had saved the dunes of Provincetown from billboards and motels and hotdog stands. As boys, the Kennedys had often visited the islands on day trips from Hyannisport aboard their father's yacht. As teenagers, they had raced their sailboats in the islands' waters. Had Jack Kennedy's Cape Cod National Seashore legislation not been enacted, virtually nothing would have been left of the Cape Cod traversed and eloquently described by Henry David Thoreau in the previous century.

Outside the Seashore area, most of Thoreau's "fawn-colored" birches and maples had been replaced by a highway lined with clam shacks and lobster eateries, antiques emporiums, motels, mini-golf ranges, and souvenir shops selling mementos of "Olde Cape Cod." The wild ducks that once had floated on the myriad ponds of the Cape were mostly gone. Its wealth of songbirds had diminished as their habitat made way for summer cottage developments and Boston bedroom communities.

As octogenarian Henry Hough's brown eyes looked out toward Nantucket Sound,

Edgartown's Dr. Daniel Fisher House, built in 1840, was the home of the founder of the nation's largest whale-oil candle factory. *Photograph by M.C. Wallo*

sparkling under the first light that September day in 1976, he mused over the tumultuous four years before. He had been too sanguine, he knew, when the Senate version of the trust bill had been passed the year before. Now that it had not been endorsed by the House Subcommittee on National Parks and Recreation, he was no longer hopeful. Ideally, the subcommittee would have passed it on to the full House Committee on Interior and Insular Affairs, but 1976 was a presidential election year. Members of Congress wanted to recess early and the bill to protect the islands was, clearly, a controversial one, requiring more time to study and revise than they wanted to spend. Richard Nixon was president; Congress was Republican and disinclined to go out of its way for the Democratic senator from Massachusetts.

For four years, the residents of Martha's Vineyard and Nantucket who were opposed to the legislation (principally wealthy landowners and those in the building trades) had made it clear they felt the bill would give the federal government too much control over local affairs. Bill supporters had insisted just the opposite: that more federal oversight should be spelled out in the legislation. And the federal government was being asked for $10 million to acquire and protect endangered land. It was too much for Congress to deal with just then. In any case, the Department of the Interior had never liked the legislation, Henry Hough knew.

So his steps were slower than usual as he and his dog left Sheriff's Meadow to follow the rest of their early morning route. It took them through one end of the shire town of Edgartown, the Vineyard's county seat, down to the harbor light. They passed familiar white-clapboard, black-shuttered captains' houses, still as imposing as when they were built for successful whalemen in the mid-nineteenth century. That was when Dr. Daniel Fisher's sperm whale candle factory had prospered on the waterfront and many an Edgartown vessel was off in the South Pacific.

Edgartown with its whaling heritage was the obvious choice to settle down in when Henry and Betty Hough had arrived on the Vineyard in 1920, the new owners of the eighty-four-year-old *Vineyard Gazette*. As a boy, Henry had been entranced by tales of the adventures of an island whaling forebear. In his adult years, conservationist and animal lover that he was, Henry recognized the tragedy of the slaughtering of the leviathan, but he still found whaling romantic enough to write two books about it.

Graham and his master crossed North Water Street just beyond the grandest of the Vineyard's whaling mansions, their widows' walks looking out onto Edgartown harbor. The pair headed down the winding lighthouse path past the little lagoon. There, some mornings, they would see a heron feeding or snowy egrets that had flown over from the little neighboring island of Chappaquiddick. Henry Hough always kept some cracked corn in his jacket pocket on his visits to the lighthouse, for a hungry Canada goose might be in need.

The harbor entrance was still that late September morning except for the chugging of a lobsterman's boat engine. The summer season, when gleaming motor yachts of fifty to a hundred feet were anchored off Cape Pogue, was over now and Edgartown harbor was returning to off-season tranquillity.

The fall wind was brisk and the sun was fully up as the balding man and his copper and white dog made their way back past the bayberry bushes and the plumes of phragmitis. The man climbed, the dog gamboled to the street just below the sprawling, turreted Harbor View Hotel.

He had managed, over the years, to keep billboards off the Vineyard, save ancient stone walls from rock crushers, limit the use of pesticides on the island, preserve historic trees. He had fought for threatened salt marshes, intelligent zoning, historic districts, and the establishment of wildlife preserves. He had wheedled, cajoled, and persuaded seasonal visitors of means to buy meadows and woods and waterfront estates in danger of falling to developers. He had made sure that a TV tower did not intrude on a pristine landscape. He had kept centuries-old houses from being felled to make way for parking lots. He had fought against trailer parks and blacktop on the island he loved. The Sheriff's Meadow Foundation he and Betty Hough had started was the forerunner in the conservation movements on the island.

In 1978, his alma mater, Columbia University, had conferred on him an honorary doctorate in Humane Letters, praising him as a "country editor, essayist, pioneer conservationist. . . . Your passionate editorials in defense of the wetlands and meadows, the wildlife and woodlands, the beaches and waters of your island home have long preceded the historical awakening to our endangered environment," the citation had read.

Thirty years earlier, in his best-selling book *Country Editor,* he had written: "For each of us, there is some corner of the world, and I rejoice that this is mine." And he had determined to spend his life preserving that corner.

As he and Graham rounded the North Water Street corner, headed up Main Street, crossed it and went down South Summer Street, he was feeling a little better. The Vineyard air in September, after the summer's traffic had gone, was refreshing and clear again. In the early morning, Edgartown still seemed, as he had once written, "far away from noise, smoke, dirt and pressure." He had always found it "a kind of solitary outpost" that nurtured peace of mind. His walk with Graham had done the trick.

The *Vineyard Gazette* sign above the white picket fence shifted slightly in the wind as he opened the front door. A few pink Betty Prior roses lingered in the dooryard. He knew the Vineyard he loved had just suffered a great loss in Congress, but, as he always said about book rejections, "Anyone who feels a rejection is a calamity had better stop writing. There is no setback that a night's sleep won't cure."

By 1972, four years earlier, Vineyard building permits were being issued at the rate of one a day. Experts were estimating that, at this rate, by 1980 motor traffic on the Vineyard in the summer would increase two and a half times and pedestrian traffic perhaps three times. An investigative team hired by county officials to study the island also had warned that, without conservation measures, Martha's Vineyard was in serious danger of suffering terminal environmental cancer. These dire predictions had led to the Islands Trust Bill proposal. Its exponents had clearly shown how quickly the Vineyard would become a second Cape Cod if no one did anything to stop it.

In what remained of his life, Henry Hough was determined to keep that from happening.

In 1939, the *Vineyard Gazette* found a permanent home on Edgartown's South Summer Street in a gray-shingled house dating from the eighteenth century. *Photograph by M.C. Wallo*

Chapter 2

This Fragile Island

The one-hundred-square-mile island of Martha's Vineyard lies five miles off the coast of southeastern Massachusetts. Shaped by glaciation at the end of the last Ice Age, the Vineyard's geology resembles that of Long Island and Cape Cod, both similarly formed. The island has ponds and bluffs, great boulders, sandy and rocky shores, barrier beaches, and a multitude of sheltered harbors. The extensive great plain in its center is one of the largest in New England, and the heath hen—an Eastern prairie chicken—thrived there until its extinction, generally thought to have been by a forest fire in 1933. Bayberries, huckleberries, and blackberries cover its moors. When Henry Hough first knew the Vineyard in the early years of the twentieth century, the Gay Head Cliffs of multicolored clay—red, black, white, yellow, and green—at its southwestern end were even then a renowned New England tourist attraction. Gay Head Indians, the Wampanoags, made up most of that town's population and welcomed tourists to an inn above the cliffs. Sheep grazed on island fields, and stone walls undulated along the field perimeters to keep them from straying.

As the name Vineyard suggests, wild grapes grow in profusion at the edge of clearings. In island woods are black, white, scarlet, and scrub oaks, pitch and white pine, sassafras, and an occasional maple. Here and there are stands of beetlebung trees. Although elsewhere the trees are called tupelo, on the island they are named for the beetles—mallets—made from their wood and used for driving bungs (stoppers) into whale oil barrels.

Arbutus and lady slippers, sweet fern and cowslips grow in damp sheltered places in spring. The fragrance of honeysuckle and wild roses perfumes the summer air, and meadows are splashed orange by butterfly weed. In fall, those fields are gilded by goldenrod, cranberries ripen in bogs, and purple beach plums, like miniature lanterns, festoon the island dunes.

The Gay Head Cliffs of multicolored clay, a National Historic Landmark, are a popular tourist attraction. *Photograph by Mark Alan Lovewell*

Today yachts of all sizes and shapes bob at harbor moorings, but in Henry Hough's early island years, three- and four-masted schooners still sailed by, laden with lumber, and fat green fishing trawlers and swordfishing boats hailed from Gay Head and Menemsha.

Vineyard shores can be rocky and wild, dramatic with boulders and headlands, and strewn with stones that rumble when the ocean breaks over them. Or they can be wide stretches of smooth golden sand where sandpipers scurry, plovers nest among the beach peas in the dunes, and fishermen cast for bluefish and striped bass. Beaches front on the protected waters of Vineyard Sound, too.

In Henry Hough's youth, beachcombers on the windswept ocean shores would find green and blue and rose-tinted beach glass, smoothed by the waves, or timbers washed from the schooners that crossed Vineyard Sound, and sometimes the wheel or even the wheelhouse of a boat gone amiss in a storm. Today, the beachcomber's treasures tend to be lobster pot buoys, occasional sea-sculpted driftwood, and pink-lined channeled whelk shells. On the edges of lagoons and great ponds, the tide may lap over a venerable horse-shoe crab shell. There are rectangular black mermaid's purses and rock weed with bubbles just waiting to be burst. Shellfishermen dig for clams and go after mussels and oysters. When Henry Hough was a boy, Irish moss was gathered along island shores and its gelatin used in puddings. Kelp was gathered, too, to be spread on gardens to enrich the soil.

Situated as it is on the Northeast Flyway, the Vineyard's woods and fields and gardens are frequented by a variety of birds: nuthatches and towhees, cardinals, goldfinches, catbirds and grosbeaks, flickers and woodpeckers, swallows and chickadees and red-winged blackbirds. Mourning doves coo and the occasional bobwhite whistles. A whippoorwill can sometimes be heard of a summer's night and a pheasant with its bright plumage will occasionally dash across a road. In Vineyard ponds, snowy egrets stand tall and Canada geese, swans, and ducks dive. Herring gulls and terns, and great black-backed gulls frequent the Vineyard's shores. Muskrats and otters play here, too. In cold winters, seals sun on offshore rocks.

The island population of white-tailed deer, raccoons and rabbits, field mice and skunks has become increasingly unpopular as the number of human residents has increased and felt the animals "encroaching" on their land.

Martha's Vineyard is the largest island off the southeastern Massachusetts coast. It consists of six towns—Oak Bluffs (once Cottage City), Tisbury (also called Vineyard Haven), West Tisbury, Chilmark, Aquinnah (formerly Gay Head), and the shire town of Edgartown. One legend has it that the Norsemen—perhaps Leif Ericson himelf—landed on the island about 1000 A.D. Some think the Italian explorer Verrazano also set foot on the island in the sixteenth century. But the first real record of a landing is that of Bartholomew Gosnold sailing from Falmouth, England, in 1602. He named the island Martha's Vineyard, presumably after his infant daughter (or possibly for his mother-in-law, who financed the voyage) and for the grapes he found. He returned to England with tales of its flora and fauna. Some scholars have speculated that William Shakespeare could have known of accounts of Gosnold's travels and set *The Tempest* on the island the explorer had described. Indeed, the plants and animals and fish that the shipwrecked Prospero found at his magic isle are to this day seen on Martha's Vineyard.

Thirty-nine years after Bartholomew Gosnold's visit, settlement rights on the Vineyard, the neighboring Elizabeth Islands, and Nantucket, twelve miles away, were bought by Thomas Mayhew, an English settler who lived in Watertown near Boston. (The rights had been given to two English lords by King Charles I.) Mayhew then called his missionary son Thomas Jr. from England to establish a settlement here. The young Mayhew befriended the Indians he found, studied their language, and taught them English as he sought to convert them. He founded a school for Indian children. In 1657, he returned to England to settle an estate matter, fully intending to be back. But his ship was lost at sea. A monument marks the spot on the Vineyard where the Indians' beloved missionary preached his last sermon and where, for years afterwards, they came and left stones in his memory.

During the American Revolution, a fleet of British men-of-war blockaded Vineyard Sound, preventing small craft from sailing to the mainland. Even so, in the beginning, sentiment tended to be Tory on the island. But as the Revolution progressed and the British began raiding the Vineyard for supplies, islanders turned against them. What is said to have been the second naval engagement of the war took place in Holmes Hole (later Vineyard Haven) harbor. A Vineyard whaleboat was rowed up to the stern of an armed British schooner one night and the whaleboat's captain threatened to blow up the ship's rudder if the schooner was not surrendered. The schooner was.

Another legendary tale of island heroism is about the liberty pole that stood where dissenters gathered in Holmes Hole. The British announced they were going to take it to use as a spar; three teen-aged girls bored holes in it, filled them with gunpowder, and blew up the pole rather than have it in the hands of the enemy. When some five hundred British troops landed on the Vineyard, they carried off ten thousand sheep and three hundred head of cattle. The British promised to pay for what they had taken, but they paid only partially even after an envoy was sent three times to London to demand compensation. During the war years, John Paul Jones landed on the Vineyard to bury one of his seamen. Toward the end of the war, Vineyarders recognized they were very vulnerable to attack on their unprotected island, and decided to be neutral.

Farming—in particular the raising of cattle and sheep—was at first the Vineyard's chief source of income, along with fishing for cod, which was salted and sent to the West Indies, and Atlantic whaling. In 1816, the Vineyard's first Pacific-bound whaleship left Edgartown and, for the next forty years, whaling brought the Vineyard prosperity. Eleven island-owned and captained whaleships plied the distant seas and one of the largest sperm oil candle factories in the world was operated in Edgartown. Stately white clapboard sea captains' mansions soon lined Edgartown's streets. Gay Head Indians crewed on the whaling vessels. Tashtego, the "harpooneer" of Herman Melville's *Moby-Dick,* was a Gay Header and the third mate of the *Pequod* was a Tisbury man. Valentine Pease Jr., master of the *Acushnet* on which Melville himself sailed, ended his days as an Edgartown coal merchant; his house remains a shire town landmark.

Henry Hough's maternal grandfather, Henry Beetle, for whom he was named, was one of these Vineyard seafaring men. At seventeen, Henry Beetle went on his first voyage; by twenty-nine, he was the captain of a whaleship in the Pacific. Between voyages, he begat children; Henry Hough's mother was the third.

Precisely when the whaling island of Martha's Vineyard became a summer resort is not known, but, in 1830, Nathaniel Hawthorne was a visitor, followed soon thereafter by the poet John Greenleaf Whittier and the statesman-orator Daniel Webster. Webster's letters describing the Vineyard's delights were quoted in advertisements promoting the island as a summer retreat by its innkeepers and real estate agents.

The 1820s and '30s were the heyday of religious camp meetings nationwide and, in 1827, the Vineyard had its first of these. A week-long Methodist camp meeting was held near the West Chop lighthouse just outside Holmes Hole harbor. In 1835, another one was held in what was then the largest grove of oaks in New England, today's Oak Bluffs. The devout put up tents during their stay; by 1851, 1,200 tents sheltered between 3,500 and 4,000 who attended Sunday camp meeting services.

In 1858, the *Vineyard Gazette*—that Henry Beetle Hough and his wife Elizabeth would buy decades later—was urging visitors of all sorts, not only the devout, to vacation on the island. The *Gazette* touted the beaches of Martha's Vineyard, nine times longer than those of its rival summer resort, Newport, Rhode Island; its cooling breezes, sailing, fishing, and its sea: "that shining yet ruffled surface of green and alternate shades of blue and glittering foam, like flowers on the crested wave," according to advertisements.

The New York Yacht Club was founded in 1846; yachting was still in its infancy. Twelve years later, bad weather forced a squadron of the New York yachtsmen bound for Nahant near Boston to put into the Vineyard. They anchored in Edgartown and a dance was held to entertain them. Martha's Vineyard was well on its way to becoming a summer resort of renown.

The tents of the camp-meeting grounds in Oak Bluffs were eventually replaced by cottages. In 1869, the annual Illuminations in "Cottage City" began, designed by a land development company to attract more buyers. One night each summer, Japanese lanterns festooned the Carpenter Gothic cottages; band concerts, fireworks, and sometimes parades added to the allure of the night. Special steamers from Falmouth and New Bedford and Nantucket brought visitors to see the decorated cottages and Illumination events. (Much of this Henry Hough recorded in his first book, *Martha's Vineyard: Summer Resort, After 100 Years.*)

In the 1870s, land-buying fever began on the Vineyard. Purchased parcels were laid out into lots and avenues and parks. Developments sprouted everywhere. A railroad was proposed to run from Oak Bluffs to Edgartown and on to the South Shore beach at Katama. The editor of the *Vineyard Gazette* exclaimed, "Build this road. . . . Katama will grow; everything else will grow, and we shall become a very Vineyard indeed." The railroad was built.

Even President Ulysses S. Grant was lured to the island for a stay of several days in August in 1871; he attended a Martha's Vineyard Camp Meeting Association gathering.

In 1876, a sprawling hotel, Innisfree, was built above the Lagoon in Vineyard Haven. Theatrical and musical personalities flocked to it. Among its guests, on a vacation with her parents, was the little girl who would become the Broadway actress Katharine Cornell, and whose own home would become a Vineyard showplace. (The house is now the property of broadcast journalist Diane Sawyer and her husband, movie producer and director Mike Nichols.) Other visiting entertainers in the Vineyard's early days as a summer resort included the diminutive General Tom Thumb and Wagnerian singer Madame Nordica (the granddaughter of a Camp Meeting Association preacher).

In the mid-nineteenth century, ornate Carpenter Gothic cottages replaced camp meeting tents in the Vineyard settlement that became known as Cottage City.
Photograph by Carol Lazar, courtesy of the Vineyard Gazette.

Ornate scrollwork adorns the porch of a Carpenter Gothic cottage in Oak Bluffs,
one of hundreds constructed in the mid-nineteenth century.
Photograph by Alison Shaw, courtesy of the Vineyard Gazette

Sunlight streams along a rural road in West Tisbury. *Photograph by Mark Alan Lovewell*

Members of the theatrical world have made Martha's Vineyard their summer getaway ever since. In Henry Hough's time, Hollywood actor James Cagney became a Chilmark gentleman farmer. Patricia Neal and her then husband, writer Roald Dahl, bought an Edgartown house. Broadway's Ruth Gordon and her director-producer husband Garson Kanin had an Edgartown summer home. Opera star Beverly Sills married a third-generation West Chop summer resident. Pop singers Carly Simon and James Taylor were Chilmark summer children. Broadway costume designer Patricia Zipprodt bought an old West Tisbury house. Shakespeare director Margaret Webster found a quiet Gay Head spot to live year-round.

Writers of stage and screen came, too, such as *Diary of Anne Frank* dramatists Frances and Albert Hackett, and playwrights Lillian Hellman and Thornton Wilder. Writers attracted writers. Novelist Pearl S. Buck had a summer home. John Hersey became a next-door neighbor of Lillian Hellman's. William Styron and his poet wife Rose lived just a few houses away in Vineyard Haven. John Updike summered in Chilmark. Young David McCullough married a fourth-generation Oak Bluffs summer dweller.

Editors and publishers, too, began to find their way to the island—Atheneum founder Hiram Haydn became a close Hough friend, as did *Ladies' Home Journal* editors Bruce and Beatrice Gould. New York newspaper notables discovered the moors of Chilmark and the cliffs of Gay Head.

Henry and Betty Hough were delighted that men and women of such caliber were enjoying their island. For the most part, the Houghs and the island's celebrated visitors, happy to have found an unspoiled holiday place, agreed that the Vineyard should be kept unspoiled. The Vineyard's early celebrities also treasured their anonymity on the island; rarely did they bring it into the public eye. It was only in the 1970s and '80s, toward the end of his life, that Hough became concerned about the attention the well known of that era drew to the Vineyard.

Today, Hough advocates revere him as the pioneer in conservation on the Vineyard. He educated, inspired, alerted, and buttonholed fearlessly in the interests of the island, they say. Thanks to the protection he spearheaded, more than a third of the island's 60,000 acres are in conservation. Environmentalists from as far away as the San Juan Islands off the Pacific coast come to the Vineyard to see how these efforts work.

Hough is not, however, without critics. They maintain that he played an important and not always unwitting role in the development he decried, by his eloquence about the Vineyard's charms not only in his books but also on radio and television when it promoted book sales.

Since Hough's death in 1985, the island of Martha's Vineyard has continued to attract the rich and famous; but today's celebrities, rather than seeking serenity and privacy on the island, seem to delight in letting the public know that the Vineyard is their vacation home. Their designer mansions sprawl on Vineyard waterfronts and crown its hills, and are pictured on the covers of national architectural magazines. Their recipes and gardens are the subjects of books. The developers Henry Hough sought to discourage in the columns of his paper have continued to build. Henry Beetle Hough would not have been well pleased.

Chapter 3

New Bedford Childhood

Henry Beetle Hough was born on November 8, 1896, on the second floor of a three-story clapboard house on Campbell Street in New Bedford, Massachusetts. His mother, Abby Louise (Beetle) Hough, who had been head nurse at New Bedford's St. Luke's Hospital, was thirty-eight; his father, George A. Hough, then city editor of the *New Bedford Evening Standard,* was twenty-eight. The house was an unpretentious one on an unpretentious street. The Hough garden was brightened in summer by the sweet briar rosebush and the dahlias that Abby Louise grew.

Across the street, an empty lot was strewn with granite slabs to be used in house foundations. It was a fine place for Henry's games with his brother George when the boys were small. Later, a house went up on the lot, another of the ordinary shingled and clapboard houses that lined the maple-shaded street.

Fences tended to separate one house lot from another. One backed up on the Hough yard and another stood between their house and the "splendid red"—as Henry described it—Conant house next door. Mr. Conant had been Henry's father's tailor in his bachelor days. That connection notwithstanding, "Old Coconut" Conant, as he was familiarly called, would shout impatiently at the boys if they played on the fence. Mrs. Conant, however, was a friend of Abby Louise's and Henry Hough remembered being quite put out when his mother scolded him for refusing to get off the fence when Mrs. Conant asked him to and for behaving "impudently," as his mother said. Other neighbors with whose children the boys played owned a woodworking mill and others a saloon.

When he was very little, Henry's mother would dress him up in a tam-o'-shanter and a blue wool coat and let him play with his shovel and toy wheelbarrow in the gutter in front of the house. Very few automobiles passed by so it was a safe place for such youthful industry. Since a hitching post and a granite mounting block stood at the curb, sometimes horse manure had to be avoided, but Henry was deft at that.

Though the Houghs' was a middle-class neighborhood, they were only half a mile away from some of the grand mansions of County Street. Just two blocks downhill was imposing St. Joseph's Hospital. There, when it was a private house, Hetty H.R. Green had been born. Her financial wizardry earned her the title the "Witch of Wall Street." When she was only six, the boys were told, she was able to read the financial pages of the paper to her astute grandfather. She grew up to invest what she inherited so cleverly that she became the richest (though not the nicest) woman in the world in the last half of the nineteenth century.

But it was not the prospect of riches that captured the fancy of either of the boys. A love of things theatrical was in their veins. Their great grandfather, Garry Andrew Hough,

Henry Beetle Hough grew up in this house at 85 Campbell Street in New Bedford. *Courtesy of George A. Hough 3d*

The infant Henry Beetle Hough. *Courtesy of Katharine Tweed and the* Vineyard Gazette

whom young Henry always wished he had known, was an actor in temperance plays and with a touring company of *Uncle Tom's Cabin*. As a newspaperman, Henry enjoyed the originality of the headline on his great grandfather's obituary in a Detroit paper: "CURTAIN DOWN. Garry Andrew Hough Has Made His Last Exit. . . . Death Came to Him This Morning . . . and Carried Him On Its Wings to Make His Entrance in a New Part on a New Stage."

When an *Uncle Tom's Cabin* company came to New Bedford, the boys' father made sure they saw it. He took them out of school to hear Sousa's band and when Buffalo Bill's Wild West Show was in New Bedford, they saw that, too. Henry admired Colonel Cody "all in white with white mane and goatee astride his beautiful white horse."

Best of all was when the circus was in town. Then George, Henry, and their father boarded the streetcar early in the morning to go down to the Wamsutta Mill railroad yard to see the circus trains unload, then uptown to watch the tents for the big top and the sideshows go up.

"The early morning feeling was mixed with smells of crushed grass, hay, animals, and brewing coffee. We watched the elephants at work pushing gaily painted wagons, boys carrying water, all the magnificent disorder," Henry recalled. In the afternoon, before the circus opened to the public, George Sr., with his newspaper credentials, could get his sons into the sideshows. Following, briefly, in his grandfather's footsteps, George Sr. had once traveled with the circus himself. And the most delicious waffle Henry Hough ever remembered eating—still uncooked on the inside—was one bought when the circus parade passed through New Bedford. When he was in his seventies, Henry was to liken life to a circus parade, but added wistfully "that you can't run a couple of blocks and watch it go past again."

Baseball games at the Athletic Field were never to be missed, either. The boys' grandfather, Dr. George T. Hough, was so inveterate a baseball game viewer that he ended up scoring for the *Morning Mercury*. And when he tired of it, he proposed that his son take on the task. That was George Sr.'s introduction to journalism. While he was still a teenager, Henry, too, was introduced to newspapering by covering baseball.

New Bedford, at the time of Henry's birth, had a population of 60,000. Whaling had declined significantly after the Civil War, though a few whaleships still anchored in the harbor and their whale oil casks, covered with seaweed to protect them from the sun, were piled up on the old wharves. On Sunday walks, always accompanied by one or another family dog, the boys' father might take them down to the wharves below Johnny Cake Hill to see what remained of whaling days. Sometimes an old whaler, partly dismantled, would lie at a wharf waiting to be sold and broken up.

But the grandeur that whaling had brought to New Bedford was still evident on many of its streets. There, the granite mansions of whaleship owners rose behind the horse chestnuts and maples. "A walk through the long avenues . . . was like a walk through the broad side of a great cathedral," Henry remembered. "Such was the beauty that inspired Melville," he wrote.

Every Sunday morning, the young Houghs attended Grace Episcopal Church on County Street, the grandest of all the streets. They sat in a back pew and left before Communion, since they had never been baptized. (Henry's bride-to-be was to discover this just before her wedding day.) During the first part of the service, Henry listened to the melodious voice of the priest reciting Morning Prayer (he even vaguely considered becoming a minister because he liked that service so much). But once the sermon was under way, his mind wandered and he plotted how he would climb on the Victorian church's remarkable High Gothic roof. Despite the churchgoing, his was not a religious upbringing. His father said that he had had more than enough church to last him a lifetime when he was a boy.

In the New Bedford of Henry's childhood, cotton mills had succeeded whaling as the principal source of income. In 1911, sixty-seven of them operated in the city and New Bedford ranked second in the country in its number of spindles—the measurement, at the time, of a city's textile wealth. Accompanying the development of the mills was an increase in population, so that by the time Henry left high school, New Bedford's population had more than doubled. He liked to remember the city then as a prosperous, exciting one. There were schooners in the harbor and bustling barges. Packet boats brought Azoreans and Cape Verdeans to be part of the workforce. Cotton was unloaded at the State Pier and steamers sailed from there to New York. The interurban trolley line went to Fall River.

In 1902, when the new sidewheeler *Uncatena* arrived from Wilmington, Delaware, for her maiden voyage to the Vineyard, the boys were taken down to see her and Henry was reassured that aboard that brand new steel-hulled vessel he would never have to worry about being seasick. Or Henry and his father might walk across the Fairhaven Bridge over the Acushnet River into Fairhaven. Then they would come back home across the Coggeshall Bridge through New Bedford's North End for a six-mile walk. If they had more time to spend, their destination would be eight miles away out on Clark's Point. There they could look out onto the blue waters of Buzzards Bay and, in clear weather, see the Elizabeth Islands in the distance. Along the Acushnet River, the city's waterway, George Sr. might talk of his Quaker mother's family and how, during the Civil War, they had helped runaway slaves escape on the Underground Railroad, many as stowaways aboard a vessel on the river.

Those Sunday walks of childhood turned Henry into an inveterate walker. "When your youth, all the way to voting age, has been lived in terms of such experience, you never lose the feel of long walks or the latent keening of your body to be out and away, one foot after the other," he wrote in his eighties when he was still walking three miles a day. "The independence is a good part of it."

George A. and Abby Louise Hough with their sons George Jr.
and Henry in their teens. *Courtesy of George A. Hough 3d*

Once home, after supper, they would gather around the lamplight in the sitting room. Abby Louise would take the mending out of her whalebone sewing box and the boys would play dominoes, or they and George Sr. would read. Books were everywhere in the house except the kitchen. George Sr. was particularly fond of Daniel Defoe and had collected his works. There were sets of Dickens and Stevenson, of course, and tales about traveling and living with gypsies by George Borrow. The boys enjoyed works like *Mr. Midshipman Easy* by Captain Marryat and Dickens's *David Copperfield* and *Oliver Twist*. Sometimes there would be peppermints to eat out of a wooden box or Henry's favorite licorice strings to nibble on.

The boys attended the Mary B. White School and the Parker Street School before entering New Bedford High School, where Henry did especially well in history and Latin. He joined the high school cadets, marching in a parade with President Taft in 1912 when he and two other presidential candidates, Teddy Roosevelt and Eugene Debs, were on the campaign trail in New Bedford. It was in high school, too, that Henry decided he was in love with his Latin teacher, Tyna Hellman. He always remembered his parting with her on that June day in 1914, the last day of high school. "How fair the world was," he recounted, "how fresh the breeze from the harbor, and how tranquil the glimpses of tree-shaded Fairhaven on the other side of the broad tidal river. Classes were over, I was free, and Miss Hellman, now more friend than teacher—a new relationship that surprised and touched me as an unexpected coming of age—gave special advice about the College Board Latin examination I was about to take."

Like every other youth's, Henry's teenage years had not always been happy ones, however. The time he passed two female classmates and overheard one remark to the other, "That Hough boy always looks so awful," had never stopped chafing. In his recollection, he wistfully continued that he had "never been a fashionplate or anything like it."

As they grew up, the boys saw more and more of their father's newspaper activities. After those initial days of scoring baseball games for the *Morning Mercury*, George Sr. had been hired as a reporter for the paper. Then he moved to its sister paper, the *Standard*, where he was to become city editor and finally managing editor. He made no bones about being a crusader, going after the police for corruption, the mayor for incompetence. He brought to light the sordid details of saloon "back rooms" where men and women drank together, "a place where the underworld seeks its unhealthful and feverish pleasures," his paper said. That campaign began after a woman was picked up by a coal barge captain in a back room and hacked to death on his barge.

George Sr. ran three times for alderman and won once. It was proposed that he run for mayor, but he declined. On election nights, the boys were always down at the *Standard* office to watch the returns.

All this made Henry politically aware at a young age. "New Bedford was an ornately and picture-squeaky corrupt city and the *Standard* was always fighting the administration, sometimes winning and usually not winning," Henry recalled. But clearly, his father's penchant for "ruckuses," as he called them, was passed on to his son, along with the resiliency to keep fighting even if one battle was lost. Although Henry's battles as editor of the *Vineyard Gazette* were principally for conservation, they could be as rip-roaring as his father's against corruption. And, like his father, even if he lost one fight, he was always ready to take on a new cause or a new opponent.

"My brother and I, when you come right down to it, grew up in a school of journalism and politics long before Joseph Pulitzer endowed the school at Columbia, and long before we ever supposed we would go to such an innovative academic-professional institution."

Henry's affection for the place of his birth—an affection nurtured by walking everywhere in its one hundred square miles, watching the seagulls diving on its waterfront, smelling its sea smells—never left him. After World War I, the textile industry started to move south and New Bedford began to die. Its historic buildings were torn down and the crusading paper of his father's day changed hands. In 1960, Henry used a New Bedford–like coastal city as the setting for his sixth novel *Lament for a City*.

"Poor New Bedford," he wrote, "which, in my childhood was still a city of great beauty, wealth and culture, has sunk into spartan and ugly urban waste. All that was magnificent has gone."

Chapter 4

North Tisbury Summers

Henry Beetle Hough's affection for Martha's Vineyard began in boyhood when he and George Jr. roamed the hills of North Tisbury together.

"If it had not been for childhood and youth there," Henry Hough wrote in 1956 to David E. Lilienthal, his friend and North Tisbury neighbor, and former Atomic Energy Commission chairman, "this pattern of years on earth would have been a lot different."

When Henry was two years old, his father bought a farmhouse just above the shore of Vineyard Sound as a summer retreat. The Vineyard was only an hour and a half away from New Bedford by side-wheeler, and the natural place for George Sr.'s family to vacation: he had known it as a boy and his father had once practiced medicine there; Abby Louise was born on the Vineyard and the couple had met and courted on the island.

Crossing the fields one day, George and Louise (sometimes she was Abby, sometimes Louise, depending upon George's mood at the moment) happened on three gray-shingled farmhouses separated by fields, thickets, and stone walls. George bought one of them, then the second, and finally the third. He had them moved and two of them put together and transformed into one house. Each summer after that, he installed his wife and children there and joined them on weekends. During the week, the boys explored the nearby hills and woods and beaches on their own.

The Vineyard getaway really began on Patriots' Day in April, a holiday commemorating the battles of Lexington and Concord in 1775. The Houghs planted their North Tisbury flower and vegetable gardens then. A month or so later, they returned for a Memorial Day holiday to see how their seeds were doing. Once school was out in New Bedford, the permanent vacation move was made.

The Hough family and their dog Jack on a summer's day in North Tisbury in the 1890s.
Courtesy of the *Vineyard Gazette*

The only thing Henry Hough didn't like about this summer home was getting there if the weather was stormy. Even though he wore a sailor suit that his mother said made him look "every inch a sailor," he always felt queasy if the crossing was rough. And it could be, once the boat was out of New Bedford harbor and had passed Palmer's Island and the Butler's Flat lighthouse and headed across Buzzards Bay toward Woods Hole. If there was a southeast wind of any strength blowing, the waves struck the vessel broadside, making it roll and shake and quiver. It didn't matter then that Henry's maternal grandfather was a whaleship captain; his grandchild invariably was seasick—a condition engraved so deeply in his young mind that never afterward did he enjoy traveling. Indeed, he remarked only half facetiously in later life, all the good sensations of travel could be had by going up to the attic, putting one's feet into a pail of cold water, and reading the *National Geographic*.

Rough seas or not, of course, there was much excitement aboard a boat. At sailing time, he covered his ears at the shrill boat whistle and waited for the bellowing call "All ashore that's going ashore," followed by the casting off of the big hawsers that moored the side-wheeler to the wharf. In his retentive mind, he stored up much of the flavor of the sea even in those young days, and drew upon those recollections many times in books that were to come.

He always enjoyed the attention from the stewardess on board to look after traveling children. She was from the Vineyard Wampanoag Indian community of Gay Head. He never forgot her kindness and for the rest of his life had a warm spot in his heart for Gay Headers. A snappily uniformed purser had an office on the main deck, and dispensed tickets and miscellaneous information about the crossing through a little window. By the time the side-wheeler had crossed Buzzards Bay and Vineyard Sound and was in the lee of the land, entering Vineyard Haven harbor, Henry's stomach usually settled down—in any but the worst of crossings—as he anticipated what lay ahead.

The family was met by horse and carriage, the luggage piled in, and off they went on the road out of town toward North Tisbury. The trip along the wooded road to the middle of the island took almost as long as the boat crossing from New Bedford. Much of it was uphill and tiring for the horse.

On sunny days, the trees arching over the road cast long shadows on it. Along Indian Hill Road, the final leg of their journey, some of the trees were curiously bent, supposedly by Indians to make a fence for their cattle. When that road ended, a narrow, stony road to the right went downhill and then up through pine and oak woods to the house where Abby Louise and her boys remained for the next three months.

George Hough Sr. had named the farmhouse Fish Hook. A colleague from the *New Bedford Evening Standard* had picked a fish hook out of a box of odds and ends when he was visiting one day. Holding it up, he had remarked that since George's house was "at the end of the line," Fish Hook would make a perfect name for it.

When they arrived, the boys took a quick look at the blue waters of Vineyard Sound a quarter of a mile below them. Then they were back at the house, climbing upstairs to George's room. From there, they could see as far away across the water as Gay Head, where the light flashed white three times and then red once. They always considered it a good omen for the summer if the first flash they saw when they looked out the window was the red one.

Then all the supplies from the city had to be unpacked. Kindling was brought in for the Glenwood range where supper was cooked, and logs to feed the three fireplaces in chilly weather.

As soon as the family was settled in, the boys went off to see what flotsam and jetsam had washed up on the North Shore during the preceding winter. There might be an oar, or enough of the remains of a boat so that they could climb in and pretend that they were at sea.

Their nearest neighbors were George and Margaret Rogers. Mr. Rogers, who had once been a mate on a whaling voyage, wore two gold hoops in his ears in the way of seafaring men. In his boathouse on the beach he kept a little boat for fall codfishing. Every November he rowed or sailed to the codfishing grounds off Noman's Land, a little island off Gay Head where Vineyarders grazed their sheep in summer. He kept some of his catch just off shore in a weighted net on four spikes, until it was time to market them. But he dried some of the cod, too, splitting them and laying them out in the sun on the roof of the boathouse. (The boys changed into their bathing suits there and it always smelled of fish and copper and twine.) The dried cod was taken into Vineyard Haven to Fischer Brothers, packed in wooden boxes, and sold under the Boat Brand name. Inspired by this example, the boys proudly labeled the Irish moss they gathered on the beach for their mother's blanc-mange "Fish Hook Brand."

Sometimes Mr. Rogers took Henry and George out fishing with him. He endeared himself to Henry by calling him Bub, which he told Henry was what whaleship cabin boys were called. (Fifty-two years later, Henry Hough would be inspired to write of valiant cabin boys and whalemen in a boys' adventure book, *Great Days of Whaling*.) Or the boys pulled lobster pots with another neighbor, Mayhew Norton. Occasionally, George and Henry were invited to go the four miles to Naushon in the Elizabeth Islands by Obed Daggett and Otis Burt, who kept their fish traps there. Afterwards, they took the catch to market on Cape Cod.

Henry tried bravely to enjoy those fishing expeditions—seasickness notwithstanding—and he remarked later in life that a day on the sound with a fisherman was way ahead of yachting in his estimation. Still, he much preferred swimming in salt water to sailing on it. He was an indefatigable swimmer, happily splashing off the beaches below Fish Hook for hours. When he was in his eighties, he was still bathing as early as April and continued to go into the water into November. (In old age, however, he was more likely to be taking his dips in the warmer waters of Edgartown than on the chilly North Shore.)

In July, the boys picked berries for their mother's homemade jam and jelly: high bush and low bush blueberries and huckleberries. The light blue dangleberries, not tasty enough

The North Shore was an inviting place for Henry (in white) and his brother, George, from their very earliest years. *Courtesy of Katharine Tweed and the* Vineyard Gazette

for their mother's cookery, were just fine for outdoor snacks. In the August berrying season, they invariably returned home with blue fingers, and arms and legs well scratched from picking in the blackberry thickets.

On early fall weekend visits, Henry and George gathered the wild grapes—some purple, some red, some so clear they were almost white—that grew all around Fish Hook. They took a pail to the cranberry bog near the shore in the hope they could pick enough to go with the Thanksgiving turkey. Once, when the whole family went to the bog together, they managed to fill a whole barrel with berries.

Henry often followed the path to the Mayhew Norton house to bring back fresh milk, sometimes straying onto the Lambert's Cove estate of William Butler (later a U.S. senator) not far through the woods from Fish Hook. Years later, when this property and all the land around it was in danger of being sold for development and Henry Hough was working to prevent it, he was to remember how Mayhew Norton had murmured that he guessed the senator wanted to own every piece of land around him.

At Fish Hook the Houghs tended some livestock, including chickens the boys raised for eggs. One summer they had three goats, Fogo, Brava, and Elizabeth (named in the bookish, historically minded Hough family for Good Queen Bess), as well as a Belgian hare called Bunny. The antics of the billy goat Fogo were particularly interesting to the boys. One day he ambled into the kitchen from the wood room behind it and then into the dining room, much to the consternation of the grown-ups, but to the great amusement of the children. They delighted in watching the hare charge boldly at Fogo and then waiting for Fogo to charge back—until the day that Fogo's horns gored Bunny fatally.

For several summers a pig and an assortment of dogs also lived at Fish Hook—a bulldog named Jack among them. He had been saved from being a pit fighting dog (dog fights were a popular New Bedford sport then) by the boys' father. George had his own pony, Phil, when he was small and when he was older a horse, Molly, that he would sometimes take down to the boat on Saturdays to bring his father home.

The boys played scrub baseball behind the house, with a game for the championship of Fish Hook before the summer ended. Henry was not happy when his brother and the housemaid, Minnie Mahoney, beat him and his father 15 to 12 for the 1906 championship.

A dark pine grove on a ridge downhill from the house was another favorite place for playing; often the boys were content just to be left alone in their own woods.

When the rain and wind beat at the windows of the old farmhouse, the boys played inside by the fire in the paneled library. Here George edited and published the Fish Hook Log, which he sold for ten cents a copy. As for Henry, who was two years younger, he diligently drew columns on a piece of paper to produce his own publication, called Doings of the Household. The boys also put on plays, as they did in New Bedford. In one of their productions, Henry acted the role of the swashbuckling Count of Monte Cristo. The boys would also ask their mother for tales of her father's thirty years at sea, inspired by the three- and four-masted schooners with billowing sails they had seen passing between the Elizabeth Islands and the Vineyard, on their way from Maine to New York with loads of lumber.

Walking the two miles to the North Tisbury post office for the arrival of the mail stage in the evening was a high point of their summer life. The horses galloped right into the village center, and other horses were likely to be tied up to the post office rail while their owners sat on the long porch and, like the Hough boys, waited for the mail to be distributed.

On their route to and from the post office, the brothers clambered over stone walls, captured caterpillars to take home to study, and tried to catch pinkletinks, the Vineyard name for the tiny tree frogs that make such a melodious sound in the swamps in spring. The boys climbed to the top of Ram's Hill where they could look out across the whole island. They stopped sometimes to lay flowers at the little pet cemetery they made in the woods.

Henry came to know every boulder and stream and hill in his North Tisbury neighborhood. And his mother delighted in telling the boys all she knew about the wildflowers they found on walks and the birds that darted and sang in their woods.

Henry kept his father informed of their various doings by mail. On a May day in 1906, when he was eight, he wrote: "Us boys got up early this morning and handled the fire before Mother came down. Then us boys played tennis and scrub without a catcher. I beat George 6 to 4. Mrs. Rogers came over with Mrs. E. Norton about dinnertime. We had consomme and rabbit for dinner. Us boys looked for mayflowers . . . but found none."

The boys' mother was also away that May, and Henry, who was particularly devoted to her, filled her in, too, with a letter: "George and I have just been on a walk. We found some boxberries and flowers. I have pretty hard work to get good writing out of this pen. . . . I miss you a good deal. We play boat and play along the shore. This pen is fearful. Lots of love and kisses. P.S. I have my hands pretty dirty."

Two years later, precocious Henry was passing on jokes to his father. "Here is a new one," he gleefully wrote in July of 1908, "which you have never heard."

> She was leaning on the rail
> Looking deathly pale
> Can't be she's looking for a whale.
> Not at all.
> To Papa's only daughter
> Casting bread upon the water
> In a way she hadn't oughter
> That is all.
>   *Anonymous*

Young Henry spent many happy hours in the Fish Hook library.
Courtesy of George A. Hough 3d

Weekends, when George Sr. arrived, meant family clambakes on the beach, hoisting the American flag on the knoll near the house, and excursions to the big rock at Indian Hill, reputedly the site of an Indian dancing field. The view from atop the rock encompassed both sides of the island.

The Houghs also picnicked on Prospect Hill in neighboring Chilmark and indulged in red and pink lemonade. One Sunday a summer, they went to Pohogonot on Oyster Pond in Edgartown where the Flynns of Fall River had a hunting camp. Young George Flynn was the same age as Henry and Tom Flynn a little younger, and they were all fast friends. Once a summer, too, they took an excursion boat to the colored clay cliffs at Gay Head and rode to the top in an oxcart driven by a Gay Header.

Sundays, after a satisfying midday dinner, often of lamb and roast potatoes finished off with Madeira cake and cheese, the whole family went to the top of a hill the boys dubbed San Juan Hill in honor of Teddy Roosevelt's 1898 victory in Cuba. There, if the wind was right, they flew their box kites.

Evenings, the family had bowls of steaming chicken chowder (one of the few dishes the adult Henry Hough ever prepared), or boiled lobsters from Mr. Rogers, or frankfurters boiled with tomatoes. Sometimes they roasted corn and potatoes in the living room fireplace and their father read to them. *Robinson Crusoe* was among his favorites.

"Those Fish Hook days and nights set one of the unending bloodstream patterns in the life of a little boy growing up," Henry Hough wrote toward the end of his life. "H.B.H. never lost the look and feeling and whole strong thread of summers and holidays in the house at North Tisbury."

Once or twice a summer the Houghs walked the three miles to George Gifford's Store in West Tisbury for a refreshing treat of ginger ale. When they needed a box of crayons or a tube of paste, the family went into Cottage City (later Oak Bluffs) or Vineyard Haven. Sometimes coming up from the boat, Henry and George's mother stopped for items of summer apparel—sneakers and caps, and, when the boys were small, waterwings and toy boats.

The family also visited Abby Louise's sisters, Addie and Emma, in Vineyard Haven. The boys' paternal grandmother, Lydia Winslow (Anthony) Hough, had a cottage on County Park in Cottage City. Of Quaker stock, she always wore black. But the boys were not put off by her apparel. They enjoyed sitting on her cool verandah shaded by a Dutchman's pipe vine, riding on the Flying Horses Carousel, and eating popcorn and ice cream. Henry never forgot the way the tar streets there became sticky and then soft in the heat of summer, and his bare feet would get stuck. Long afterwards, when he was writing editorials opposed to the black-topping of island roads and parking lots, he would refer to that hot melted tar.

The fall when Henry became ten, the boys and their mother stayed at Fish Hook late into the fall, almost to the end of October. The family had delayed the start of their

Vineyard sojourn because young George had contracted spinal meningitis at the end of the New Bedford school year. The fresh air of the island, everyone hoped, would help in his recuperation. That fall, because he was supposed to rest, George stayed home from school, but Henry was sent down the Indian Hill Road to the one-room Locust Grove School.

Several youngsters came over the North Shore hills to attend the school, and Henry joined them on their walk "past the towering oak that produced sweet acorns." Nineteen pupils from five to twelve were all taught by one teacher. Because of the distance home, the children took their lunches with them and ate them beside the brook below the school, or, once, on the sandy top of a nearby glacial esker. Budding naturalist Henry loved these long walks and picnics and wrote in the Fish Hook logbook that he had never before had such a good time.

With its fields, a swamp, a bog, and a brook, and its fine beech trees, maples, oaks, and an occasional holly, and its sweeping shoreline, the North Tisbury of his childhood was one of the loveliest parts of the Vineyard, Henry always thought.

Six decades later, when Martha's Vineyard had become a popular summer resort and developers were willing to pay anything for property, Henry and George gave some of the Fish Hook acreage they had inherited to Sheriff's Meadow to be part of today's Cedar Tree Neck Wildlife Sanctuary. Similarly, Henry talked the heirs of Obed Daggett into selling the land they had inherited at a price far below market value so it could be part of the sanctuary. Having done that, Henry shamelessly solicited money from other conservation-minded friends and acquaintances to buy it. The effort kept 170 acres of wooded shore rising above Vineyard Sound just the way it was in the days when Henry and George would come back with a load of scup and blackfish from fishing with Obed Daggett.

Chapter 5

The Columbia Years

In 1912, Columbia University's new School of Journalism opened, founded by *New York World* editor and publisher Joseph Pulitzer. His idea of what a journalist should be reflected the views of *New Bedford Evening Standard's* veteran editor George A. Hough Sr.

"A journalist is a lookout on the ship of state," Pulitzer had written. "He notes the passing sail, the little things of interest that dot the horizon in fine weather. He reports the drifting castaway whom the ship can save. He peers through fog and storm to give warning of dangers ahead. He is not thinking of his wages or the profits of his owners. He is there to watch over the safety and the welfare of the people who trust him."

Young George Hough, youthful editor of his own Fish Hook Log, had shown an interest in following in his journalist father's footsteps. George Sr. proposed that George Jr. attend Columbia University's new school. For the first two years, the education was general—in history, philosophy, languages, politics, economics, science, English and American literature, and composition. The third year offered more writing and reporting; during the fourth year, students were placed in a regular city newsroom atmosphere, sent out on assignments, and trained in editing and rewriting.

Young George Hough liked what he found at Columbia—not only academically but also socially. Whenever he could get to Fish Hook the following summer, he talked enthusiastically to Henry about the excitement of New York City and what he was learning. (Most of the time he stayed in New Bedford that first summer, hard at work for his father on the *Standard.*)

Henry was scheduled to graduate from New Bedford High School the following February, and would have to wait another half year before college. Impatient George Sr. thought that would be a waste of time, and decided his younger son should simply forego his high school diploma and take the College Board examinations to try to get into Columbia early. Seventeen-year-old Henry Hough dutifully did as he was asked. "My own destiny," he wrote later, "might have followed wherever I was dropped. I experienced no 'call.'" Almost as soon as his sons had been born, however, their "benevolent despot" father, as Henry Hough frequently described George Sr., had decided they would both uphold the journalism tradition.

Henry bade farewell to his high school teachers and took the College Boards. He did well in Latin and German and adequately in everything else except advanced English composition—an obvious prerequisite for entering the journalism school. To correct that deficiency, Miss Muriel Kinney from Manhattan was hired as his tutor and moved in with the Houghs that summer at Fish Hook.

In September, Henry accompanied his brother to the city to take the entrance exam for the journalism school. While he waited for the appointed day, he explored the campus and sent postcards to his aunts on the Vineyard. At the journalism school library, he met a classmate of his brother's named Irwin Edman, "shy, coloring a little, the flush showing in his unpigmented fairness," Hough recalled after Edman had become a renowned philosopher.

For his advanced-English examination, Henry wrote three essays: "Edward III," "Addison, Pope and Steele as Satirists,"and "The Pathetic in Dickens." Thanks to Miss Kinney's help, he passed with a grade of 85—almost unheard of for a student entering Columbia;, the usual grades were 35 or 40. So it was that he became a member of the Pulitzer School's Class of 1918.

Like his brother, Henry Hough fell in love with New York. He liked the lofty buildings and the traffic on the mighty Hudson River as he walked under the elms in Riverside Park. At night, he watched the sky across the river at Palisades Park illuminated by the lights of the swooping Ferris wheel and the roller coaster. Sometimes, for a better view, he walked out onto the Columbia Boathouse pier. He always remembered the Pabst Beer sign over Harlem and the Hell Gate Bridge.

Miss Kinney introduced her pupil to the cultural side of her native city, taking him to Greenwich Village to a Sicilian marionette show, a street festival where chestnuts were roasted and confetti showered on the crowd, and to the latest movies.

Emboldened by this introduction, Henry, on his own, went to see Bizet's opera *Carmen* in a theater on Central Park West and visited Grant's Tomb and the Museum of Natural History. Later, in a whimsical moment, he was to propose Grant's Tomb as the site for a reunion of his class.

He lived most of the time in Furnald Hall, the newly constructed men's dormitory. There, in time, young though he was, he became chairman of the governing board. He was courted by several fraternities, but declined to join because, growing up, he had been taught that fraternities were undemocratic. He was also president of his class. Though he

Elizabeth Wilson Bowie
from Uniontown, Pennsylvania,
at the Pulitzer School of
Journalism. *Courtesy of
George A. Hough 3d*

would not, as his father had done, run for public office in later years, what he learned about politicking at Columbia would prove useful in the small-town life he was to embrace. Henry numbered among his friends Max Schuster, who, at the head of Simon & Schuster years later, would publish one of his books.

Henry took to the school with enthusiasm, in particular to the teaching of Walter B. Pitkin, who had moved from the department of philosophy to the journalism school. In later life, Henry frequently referred to a dog-eared copy of Pitkin's autobiography *On My Own.*

"Pitkin quickened me as few others have ever done," Henry Hough recalled in later years. "I was galvanized by him. His spirit runs through me," he added.

"Rolling out sentences between lips that relished every clear transmission of thought into language, Pitkin covered the history of philosophy, modern psychology, and a dash of logic, which, if it accomplished nothing more, would at least aid a young reporter to smell

Yeoman first class Henry Hough posed for a picture during his World War I service in Washington with the Office of Naval Intelligence. *Courtesy of George A. Hough 3d*

a non sequitur in the cross-examination of a witness at a murder trial," editor Hough told interviewer Everett Allen decades later.

Above all, Henry Hough never forgot that Pitkin had taught that "the human mind is not a simple bureau of truth. The working of it is colored by various things. No individual can in any manner whatsoever discount his own biases in dealing with everything." When Hough became the editor of the *Vineyard Gazette,* he readily accepted the fact that he was biased in favor of preserving Martha's Vineyard. That bias, he knew, affected everything he wrote and he did not feel guilty about it.

At the end of the first half year, Hough had earned B+ in English, B in French, A- in history, B+ in journalism, and Bs in philosophy and politics. But one paper he had written for Pitkin had earned him only a C- and the comment that "you write glibly, but without the slightest indication of having grasped what this is all about." With that comment, Hough said, he grew up overnight. He would not be a frivolous, superficial writer.

In those Columbia years, the young man from New Bedford managed to go frequently to musical events (which cost him nothing because he was on the staff of the dormitory weekly) and to theater. Years later, when he became friends with Katharine Cornell, he was pleased he could tell her with what admiration he had watched her on stage in his student days.

As Columbia turned him into a reporter and his classmates elected him to college office, he began to lose some of his shyness, too. When an invitation to Tolstoy's son Ilya to speak at the university was rescinded on political grounds, Henry Hough was the spokesman for the resolution decrying the university's suppression of freedom of thought and expression. In 1916, when Charles Evans Hughes and Woodrow Wilson were running against each other for the presidency, Hough joined the College Men's Wilson League. He led several classmates in soapbox harangues at Columbus Circle; his message was that electing Hughes would lead to war, but choosing Wilson would mean peace. When Wilson was elected, he remembered, "we felt great. But within three months we were at war. Civilization had not been saved after all." He also covered assignments for the journalism school's laboratory newspaper, *The Blot.*

From time to time during the school year, he would write New Bedford–related stories about New York for his father's paper. In the summers he began his real newspaper career working for his father. Several assignments took him to the Vineyard. On one, covering Governor's Day in the Oak Bluffs Camp Ground, he happened upon lieutenant governor Calvin Coolidge enjoying the fresh air on a hotel porch between scheduled events. The lieutenant governor noticed the earnest young reporter at the opposite end of the porch and asked him if he had all the information he needed. "This is a complete and true account of my private meeting with a future President of the United States," the fledgling reporter wrote. At Columbia, he became the campus correspondent for the *Boston Transcript,*

New York American, and the *Christian Science Monitor.* When, however, somewhat tongue-in-cheek, he sent the *Monitor* a story about the expansion of the university's new medical school, his offering was not appreciated.

In 1917 war was declared and Columbia president Nicholas Murray Butler warned that the freedoms of speech, assembly, and publication that he had frequently deplored in the past on campus, but had felt obliged to tolerate, would no longer be permitted. Three Columbia students, including one from the journalism school, were arrested as "anti-draft" plotters. Far from being intimidated by their arrest, Henry Hough joined the Columbia Anti-Militarist League. Professors resigned in protest against the university's cancellation of the right of free speech; some were fired. Journalism students went to meetings to hear anarchist Emma Goldman. In their New Bedford years, the Hough boys had learned from their father the importance of taking a stand for one's beliefs—even when unpopular. At Columbia, as both faculty and students chafed under the edicts of the notoriously authoritarian university president, their father's advice was reinforced.

That year Hough was given an assignment he never forgot. He was to write a letter of advice to Mrs. Mary Publisher, a supposed widow who had inherited her husband's paper. She knew nothing about editing and publishing a newspaper, the assignment said. After Henry himself became an editor and publisher, he would often think back to one sentence of that letter he had written: "My dear Mary. . . . You ask if every editor and manager must give up everything to his newspaper. Without hesitation, my answer is in the affirmative."

Meanwhile, both George and Henry Hough had found romantic interests at the journalism school. George had become smitten with a classmate of Henry's from California, Clara Sharpe. Henry, on his way to cover a night court story for *The Blot,* had stopped at a soda fountain and struck up a conversation there with down-to-earth Elizabeth Wilson Bowie, a doctor's daughter from Uniontown, Pennsylvania. Two years older, she had earned her BA at Wells College in New York State, and then studied at Barnard before entering the journalism school's class of '19. She had been the editor of her Wells paper.

Henry liked her earnestness. She had marched down Fifth Avenue in a woman suffrage parade and her mother, Henry learned, had been active in the Children's Aid Society of Western Pennsylvania, helping find homes for hundreds of orphans. Betty Bowie had that same compassion, Henry Hough felt. And, like his mother, Abby Louise, Betty Bowie brooked no nonsense from anyone. But she had a softer side, too. He found that they shared a love of animals and of nature. She talked of her horses and of collie dogs and of the woods at Pine Knob, Pennsylvania, where she had spent childhood summers. He described Martha's Vineyard's North Shore. Occasionally, they would share Chinese food at Lock Yin on Broadway and 101st Street or a table d'hote dinner for forty cents on Claremont Avenue—with finger bowls. He liked Betty's bright blue eyes and abundant dark hair, too, but he hesitated to say so.

"One shouldn't show admiration for the opposite sex lest one be considered fresh in Columbia days," he later recalled, adding that this inhibition continued long after that.

His pacifist sentiments notwithstanding, at the close of his final year at Columbia Henry Hough decided to enlist when he learned that the Office of Naval Intelligence in Washington was looking for qualified journalists. (As a Navy journalist, his assignments would be shore-side and he would not have to cope with seasickness.) So he and Marshall "Bishop" Beuick of the class of '19 took the subway down to Chambers Street and volunteered. Once they were accepted, there was a farewell dinner and "wake," as he called it, at Lock Yin's.

In 1978, Columbia University honored Henry Beetle Hough, class of 1918, with a doctorate in humane letters as a country editor, essayist, and pioneer conservationist.
Courtesty of Columbia University Office of Public Information

Early in March, Henry Hough joined university friends in the Office of Naval Intelligence in Washington as a yeoman, first class; more were to come. Although the work was dull, the young man from small-city New England found himself thoroughly enjoying the capital. As in New York, he attended plays; once he and the president and Mrs. Wilson were in the same theater. Despite his disenchantment with his one-time hero for not keeping the country out of war, he was impressed to be near him.

Thin young man that he was, Hough filled up frequently on wheat cakes, ham, and eggs at Child's Restaurant on Pennsylvania Avenue. Clara Sharpe, his brother's future wife, worked for the Department of Agriculture. Clara, Henry, and Bishop Beuick picnicked in the Washington countryside and had their pictures taken in a canvas PT boat in a Pennsylvania Avenue studio specializing in colorful backdrops for tourist photos.

In June, Hough obtained a leave to attend his Columbia graduation. All members of his class who had enlisted in their senior year automatically received a degree, so not many of his classmates actually attended the ceremony. But it was important to Henry to be there. He and classmate Minna Lewinson had written a "History of the Services Rendered to the Public by the Press in 1917"—an account, mainly, of what the press had done in the war effort. Their paper had won one of the newly established Pulitzer Prizes. Henry, standing out in his Navy whites among the black commencement robes, was proud to accept his award and his LittB. His father and mother were just as proud to see him receive them. Henry and Minna shared the $1,000 Pulitzer award; Henry's money went into Liberty Bonds. Not so many years later, it would help to pay bills at the *Vineyard Gazette*.

"Those June days in New York—commencement, reunions, a round of pleasurable activity—remain enshrined in one of the rarest glows of my lifetime," he later wrote. "I even showed a pretty girl how to tie a Navy bluejacket's neckerchief, my arms necessarily around her shoulders. . . .

"On the final afternoon I sat at my old desk in the Journalism city room and wrote a letter to Beuick on a sheet of copy paper, recounting some of the great events. But I was referring to my whole Columbia and New York career when I added with deep emotion, 'It's all over. I shall never be so happy again.'"

And those memories never faded. Henry Hough did not forget the Pulitzer School of Journalism at Columbia, nor did the university forget him. In 1942, the School of Journalism honored him with its first annual award for making his newspaper "perhaps the best known country weekly in America. . . . He has kept alive the idea of the simple life and the notion that 'place' preserves our spiritual and physical wellbeing," the citation read. In 1978, Columbia University honored him with a doctorate of humane letters.

For his part, in 1968, Henry established a George A. Hough Scholarship in newspaper journalism in memory of his father.

Chapter 6

"Apologist Extraordinary for Steaks"

Henry's Navy leave to attend his graduation was long enough to allow him to return to the Vineyard for a happy two days at Fish Hook. It was the first time he had been back in almost a year. The pansies and the early roses were in bloom in his mother's garden. Huckleberry bells in the woods promised that there would be a good berry crop in July. He walked down to the beach with an eye to a swim, but the water was still too cold for serious bathing. On Sunday, the fog and rain rolled in; Henry and his father talked about Henry's future after the war. Henry said he didn't know what he wanted to do, but he was interested in what options he might have. Then, early Monday, he headed back by boat to New Bedford and the long train ride to a steamy Washington.

The temperature was more than 114 degrees when he emerged from Union Station and the young Massachusetts man yearned for the cool fogginess he had left behind. He had not been back long when rumors began to circulate at Naval Intelligence that sailors were being sent overseas to man naval guns on the Western Front. Henry and Beuick, fed up with the midsummer Washington heat and bored with the dreary job that kept them tied to mimeograph machines, wondered if the work they were doing couldn't be handled just as well by some of Washington's young women. If they could find satisfactory replacements, the young men speculated, then they could go where the fighting was, and that would be the patriotic thing to do. As it turned out, Beuick got sea duty, but Henry stayed in Washington. He did get another leave in August, though, when George married Clara Sharpe at the Cathedral of St. John the Divine in New York. George, by that time, was in the Army, and a happy circumstance brought both him and his bride to Washington after their honeymoon.

Henry escaped downtown Chicago's summer heat in peaceful Jackson Park.
Courtesy of Katharine Tweed and the Vineyard Gazette

During Henry's year in Chicago, he and Dudley, who frequently came out from New York, took refuge from the heat of the downtown in spacious Jackson Park. Frederick Law Olmsted had laid out the park with lagoons and wooded islands and plantings to be the site for the 1893 World's Columbian Exposition; Henry remembered seeing his father's pictures of the fair. The park offered a welcome contrast to the rest of the steamy, bustling city and Henry reveled in its greenery and the peacefulness on the water when he and Dudley canoed together on one of the lagoons. They also spent an icy January 1 in below-zero temperatures walking the soaring Indiana sand dunes that stretch for twenty-five miles between Gary and Michigan City, some rising more than a hundred feet; Henry never forgot their "majesty and character." Through an old friend of his father's, baseball-loving Henry managed to get into the 1919 World Series, which also helped make Chicago bearable.

Clean Copy, the School of Journalism alumni publication, described Henry that year as "Apologist Extraordinary for dollar-and-a-half steaks." That description didn't please him particularly, but the publication went on to say that "before his sojourn with Washington's oceanless Navy, Hank had been known as a fiction writer of promise." And Henry Hough still hoped that after the ordeal of the meat packing institute and a few other money-making jobs, he would, indeed, be a writer one day.

Henry and "Pen" Dudley remained lifelong friends, with Pen bringing his wife, Hermine, and their two daughters to the Vineyard's Cedar Tree Neck many summers. Though Henry and Pen saw each other only occasionally in later years, they corresponded with regularity and, in times of need, Pen provided emotional support to Henry, and, later, to Betty Bowie.

Pen Dudley was the first person Henry knew who had been treated by a psychoanalyst. Years later, in the 1950s, when Betty suffered severely from depression, she wondered if she should seek an analyst's care. Pen encouraged this. Betty's analyst gently explained that what she was calling depression "has some relationship to the way you have treated yourself in the course of a lifetime, principally of the things that you have not done just for the pleasure and satisfaction of them and of yourself. Sometimes it helps," he said, "to be philosophical and to recall that at the time we developed inhibitions and enforced them, we did so to avoid what might have been unendurable anxiety." The defenses Betty had erected, he went on to say, had, at least, enabled her to go on through life without any major disaster. She was able to accept that, and the depression passed. In 1958, at the analyst's death, she wondered how she would manage without him; Pen's understanding was again a great consolation. Also in that year, after Henry's novel *The New England Story* did not receive the critical acclaim he and Betty had hoped for, Pen Dudley wrote that having the book selected by the Literary Guild was no small achievement, and he reminded the couple—then in their thirty-eighth year as co-editors of the *Vineyard Gazette*—of how much they had accomplished with their combined talents. The letter was long treasured.

The Dudley friendship notwithstanding, in those Chicago days Henry yearned to be back east. He gave Lake Michigan short shrift in comparison with Vineyard Sound. He didn't think much of the *Chicago Tribune,* though it called itself "the world's greatest news-paper." A career in the Midwest with the meatpacking industry clearly was not right for the grandson of a Vineyard whaling captain. Henry missed the island where he had spent such splendid summers. He missed the salt smell of the sea and the pungent fragrance of sweet fern. He missed the peeping of the pinkletinks on spring nights and the whistle of bob-whites. And he missed Betty Bowie.

Of the two of them, Betty was having the much better time. Sent—in a raging bliz-zard—to Worcester by the *New Bedford Evening Standard,* she interviewed Irish political leader Eamon De Valera, in the United States to raise money for Irish independence. She accompanied three-time presidential candidate William Jennings Bryan when he visited New Bedford on the campaign trail.

She was also assigned a story on Martha's Vineyard and was invited on at least one week-end to enjoy the warmth and comradeship of Fish Hook by her boss George Hough and Abby Louise. A woods lover from her Pennsylvania childhood, Betty took with enthusiasm to the North Shore and happily walked the Hough cocker spaniel, Queequeg, in the scrub oaks and pines, Queequeg chasing rabbits and squirrels while Betty looked for birds. The way Betty bonded with Queequeg, a favorite of George Sr.'s because the dog ate his cigar ashes and enjoyed sips of his beer, helped endear her to her managing editor.

Only occasionally that year did Henry Hough go back east and have the chance to renew the acquaintance with Betty that had blossomed on the sidewalks of New York in the spring of 1919. "But the trips were brief and the partings by no means as sweet as such part-ings are supposed to be," Henry remembered later. The courting had to be by mail—but, in many respects, that was easier for the insecure, awkward-with-women young man and the standoffish, intellectual, and successful young woman reporter. Betty Bowie had thrived under George Sr.'s tutelage on the *New Bedford Evening Standard.* There might still be doubt in Henry's mind about his future. There was none in hers. If she and Henry became a couple, there must be a newspaper of their own in their future.

Chapter 7

A Most Excellent Wedding Present

On Patriots' Day in 1920—the day in April when the Hough family opened Fish Hook each year—Henry Hough and fiancee Betty Bowie first visited the offices of the *Vineyard Gazette.* She was twenty-six; he was twenty-four. For the next forty-five years, it would be the center of their lives. The population of the Vineyard in 1920 was under 5,000; the circulation of the *Gazette,* which was to be their wedding present from Henry's father after their June wedding, was 600.

The young couple had hoped for a larger weekly newspaper that might, in time, make money for them. They even had looked in the hills of eastern Pennsylvania that Betty had so loved as a child. But anything more substantial also would have cost more. However, Henry did have island forebears and the memories of those magical North Tisbury summers of his childhood. And his mother had told his father she would like her younger son closer than Chicago or Pennsylvania.

As for Betty, when she had visited the island on her assignment from the *New Bedford Evening Standard* the previous fall, the Vineyard had won her over with its peacefulness, the absence of clanging trolleys and trains, the wind and the water so often within sight and sound.

And there was the conversation she had overheard soon after she arrived, riding on Chester Pease's bus from the Oak Bluffs dock to Edgartown, about the elm trees condemned to make way for a movie theater.

"A distinguished looking gentleman and a woman whose pretty face did not detract from the vigor of her personality," were discussing the elms, she remembered. "I had never been particularly tree-conscious," she later wrote, "perhaps because I spent my summers on a Pennsylvania mountain top where we counted trees by the hundreds, even thousands, among them that most beautiful of trees, now as dead as the heath hen, the American chestnut. But somehow or other the situation which shook the voices and was reflected on the faces of my companions as we bowled along over what I was soon to know as the Beach Road—that picture-book ride on a lumbering bus—penetrated some vital spot of my own personality, beginning my transformation into one who would gladly sacrifice a street or a building or 100 telephone poles, or telegraph lines, or even a few heads, if the fate of a tree was involved."

The bus had trundled along past the blue-green-violet waters of Nantucket Sound, "and I was already an island convert before I reached my destination."

She didn't know then, but would soon, that her employer and father-in-law-to-be, George A. Hough Sr., had always longed to own the *Gazette* himself. If he had his life to live over again, the city newspaperman had told the couple when they announced their intention of marrying and buying a small newspaper, he would spend it with the *Vineyard Gazette*. That being out of the question for him at his age, he would, instead, buy it for them.

The day Betty and Henry went together to see their new acquisition was a glorious warm and sunny one. The serious, slender young man and the young woman with her fresh complexion sat out on the deck of the boat and an ecstatic Betty flung open her blue dolman in the warm breeze.

"All boats looked much alike to me, " she later recalled, "but all meant adventure and even hazard to my inland soul."

They took the bus from Vineyard Haven to Edgartown, the county seat and the home of the *Gazette*. The office was above the grocery store on Main Street and reached by an outside staircase. It was dingy and cluttered when Henry and Betty climbed up to it that April morning. But when they looked out the window, they saw the elm trees that had not been felled welcoming spring with their canopy of light green leaves.

And despite its shabbiness, as Henry was to recall later in his book *Country Editor,* "the whole shop . . . was dignified as few establishments are dignified. Its sheafs of proofs, its worn and battered fixtures, its printing specimens pasted on the walls—all were part of a disorder which went to make up, if not some kind of orderly sum total, at least the visual evidence of a Purpose." More pronounced than anything else, Henry remembered, was the smell—"a blend of ink and dust and time, not strong but inescapable, mysterious, elusive."

The *Gazette* office would move, in time, to its own building—its final home the eight-room Captain Benjamin Smith House, built by a commander of the militia on the Vineyard during the Revolution. It stood just off Main Street on South Summer Street. There, lindens and horse chestnuts shaded the street in summertime and rambler roses climbed white picket fences and gently perfumed the air. But inside there was always that same "mysterious, elusive" smell of ink and dust and time, and Henry and Betty Hough would not have had it any other way.

The newlywed Henry Beetle Houghs in 1920. *Courtesy of Katharine Tweed and the* Vineyard Gazette

and "tried things that angels would never have thought of attempting," Betty wrote. But Marchant always stood by their side.

The *Gazette*'s founder had, in his day, written a job description for the career they had just begun. The young Houghs read it that summer, but were not deterred by it.

"Ah, it is the life of lives," Marchant wrote of the country newspaper editor. "The confessions of an opium eater would be nothing to his confessions. He is a man of all work, a miscellaneous personage, all the way up from a devil to a gentleman. He knows, or should know, everybody and a little of everything. He is in the world and out of the world, and lives in the past, the present and the future. He must sometimes see and not seem to see—sometimes hear and not seem to hear. . . . Indeed, an editor must be all things to all men, or all men will be nothing to him."

Chapter 8

The Young Editors

For a while after the Houghs' arrival in Edgartown, the newspaper stayed in its old quarters above the Corner Market, looking down on Main Street. In the small entry, current *Gazette* copies were kept on file. Behind it was a cubicle that served as the new editors' newsroom, equipped with a walnut roll-top desk and an applewood table always heaped high with mail. The Houghs shared one typewriter. In those early days Henry spent much of his time getting acquainted with townspeople, soliciting advertising, and, at press time, assisting in production.

Behind an opening in the newsroom, partly hidden by a tasseled curtain, was the back shop where the paper was printed, crammed with racks and cases of type and printing presses. A job press, for invitations and calling cards, had to be pedaled; a Seth Adams hand press printed proofs; and the hand-cranked Fairchild press produced the *Gazette*.

The Fairchild required four people to run it. One—sometimes Henry—had to turn the crank slowly and carefully; another fed the paper into the press. The third person straightened the sheets of paper and turned them over to be printed on the other side. The fourth, Charles Marchant himself, cajoled the machinery, regulated the ink supply, and applied oil when needed to assure a smooth press run.

Henry enjoyed the physical labor of the back shop, but more intellectually and socially challenging tasks needed his attention. He would bicycle around town to gather ads and news, stopping to chat with a potential advertiser or a good news source, or when he was hailed by someone eager to get acquainted with the new editor. At the same time, Henry was also writing the paper's editorials, and he did so as long as he lived.

Meanwhile, Betty was throwing herself into reporting and editing. From then on, these functions would consume her. In time, Henry, whom his Columbia classmates had called "a fiction writer of promise," would make book-writing his priority, but Betty's was always to be the *Gazette*. Her ability as an editor linked with his as a writer would bring the *Gazette* national renown. "I think she was the only person I ever knew who could take prose sentences and unscramble them and make them say just what I meant them to say," New York University professor and sometime *New York Times* writer John Carr Duff said. "What remarkable talent she had as an editor."

Betty Hough stimulated and soothed town correspondents and read all their copy. She took stories over the telephone, reviewed books, and covered court ("largely because it bores Henry so," she said) as well as various meetings and social events. She also read proofs, changed addresses, and did bookkeeping. This "inlander" from Pennsylvania would even cover yachting eventually. She confessed, however, that she knew nothing about it and was delighted when the staff expanded and she could pass the beat on to someone else. "I have no hobby other the *Gazette* and collie dogs," she would write some years later in the *Wells College Chronicle*, the publication of her alma mater.

Both Houghs enjoyed covering town meetings in their early *Gazette* days. In those more tranquil times, the meetings often began in the morning, with voting on routine articles. Matters for debate usually came up after a luncheon recess.

"They were homely issues for the most part, small in scale, characteristic of the old Vineyard which would soon pass with the last of the soil-grown and sea-grown patriarchs," Henry later wrote. But it was not long before there began to be a change. At the Edgartown town meeting of 1921, a modern issue caused a furor. The incensed women of the town— by three votes—succeeded in overriding a finance committee recommendation that the street lights not be left on all night.

Another major event of 1921, covered by Betty, was the opening of the barrier beach— a narrow strip of sand that separated Edgartown's Katama Bay from the Atlantic Ocean. The channel was needed to improve the circulation of water and of nutrients that, in turn, would improve the scallop and quahog beds in the bay. Forty years earlier, an attempt to make such an opening by the U.S. Army Corps of Engineers had failed. Many were skeptical about success this time, but the town had received a small state grant for the project and put Captain Antone King, a local who had been born in the Azores, in charge. As Betty described it:

"A few minutes before 10 o'clock this morning, an opening as narrow as a little girl's hair ribbon was driven across the beach, and the placid waters of Katama Bay began their exit to the ocean. Minute by minute the break widened, assisted by the efforts of four teams of horses dragging scoops, and the workers standing hip deep in water to loosen the sand. An hour after the opening the channel was 20 and 30 feet wide."

For a while after the Houghs' purchase of the newspaper, its printing went on much as it had. The *Gazette* had a small five-column page and was never more than eight pages;

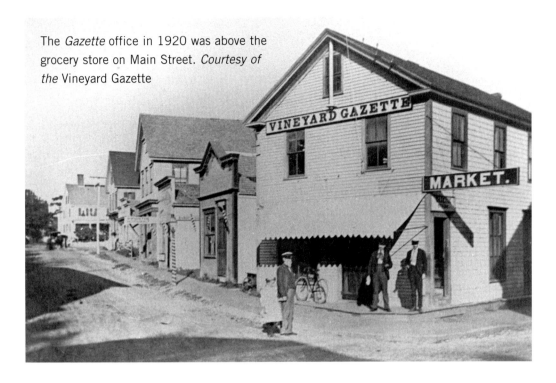

The *Gazette* office in 1920 was above the grocery store on Main Street. *Courtesy of the* Vineyard Gazette

only four could be printed at a time. Marchant ran the back shop, as he had, with his daughter and another young woman; they both set the type by hand, painstakingly picking individual letters out of a partitioned tray of type, or "job case," all week long. After the press run, each letter or character had to be put back into its proper compartment in the case for use in the next issue. Because there was not enough type in the job cases to print more than a few columns of "live" text, much of what appeared in the *Gazette* had to be boilerplate supplied by a national syndicate—pre-set accounts of the life of the South African ovenbird, for example, or of trees in the Sahara or adventures in Baffin Land.

Marchant's advertising rate of ten cents an inch would not produce enough income for the newspaper when two more people joined the staff. The Houghs were advised by advertising experts, acquaintances of Henry's father, to raise the rates to thirty-five cents an inch. After all, the enthusiastic young editors were bringing new life to the paper. But Betty (who had the better head for figures of the two) calculated that even if every inch of the *Gazette's* eight pages was devoted to ads—with no news space at all—its total annual income still would be only $12,000 with increased ad rates. That simply wasn't enough money, she pointed out—even for the most idealistic of journalists. Also, within three weeks of the Houghs' arrival, the landlord had raised the *Gazette* office rent and one of the typesetters had requested more money.

Henry pedaling down Edgartown's Main Street on *Gazette* business. *Photograph by Gretchen Van Tassel, courtesy of the* Vineyard Gazette

Henry mulled over the problem. He found only one answer. He and Betty must print a larger paper, and more of them. But to do that, they would have to replace hand typesetting with a mechanical typesetter, so they could print more fresh local news, instead of boilerplate, and attract more readers. And they would need to buy a press that was not hand-fed and hand-cranked.

Meanwhile, the newlyweds had moved to their temple-like white house with its imposing pillars. That first fall and winter were relatively mild and they managed to keep warm enough with a living room fireplace, a kitchen range, and a heater in the dining room. But it was chilly upstairs in their bedroom, and in the following winter, which was colder, they had to move to the parlor for sleeping. It was just as well that, when they finally came home at night, after a twenty-five-cent bowl of haddock chowder or beef stew at Captain St. Clair Brown's restaurant near the newspaper office, they were so tired they went to bed immediately. When they had dreamed of their weekly paper-to-be during their honeymoon at Mohonk, they had never envisioned the labor it would require.

Each day, subscribers' mail was acknowledged, and advertisers were nudged into paying bills. Just at deadline time, the town correspondents would climb up the stairs to drop off their handwritten news of the week—and then stay and talk. Ministers arrived with church notices. The women of the Want-to-Know Club (a small group of island women who met monthly for tea and a prepared talk by one of their members) came to enlist the new editors' support. Dissatisfied advertisers complained about the placement of their ads. Other complaints were aired at the office too, not necessarily about the *Gazette*, but about the weather, the poor scallop crop, the boats to the island, the summer visitors, the new postmaster.

In addition, the business still included job printing of invitations, greeting cards, and church bulletins. Working with the demanding and often short-tempered printing customers required endless patience; Charles Marchant had a great deal of it, Henry some, and Betty absolutely none. They decided to get rid of the job printing, even though it brought income, and to concentrate on the newspaper only. Henry approached the publisher of the *Martha's Vineyard Herald,* the Oak Bluffs paper that had welcomed him so warmly on his arrival in Edgartown. He offered him all of the *Gazette*'s job printing business and equipment in exchange for his newspaper. The *Herald* publisher agreed, as long as the Houghs paid him for the paper as well. Pleased with the prospect of getting rid of both the job printing and the competition, Henry and Betty secured a bank loan and bought the *Herald.*

That left the *News* in Vineyard Haven as the remaining competition. The owner had recently come into an inheritance and, for a price, he was also willing to quit the field. The *Gazette* was the island's only newspaper until the 1970s. Then, in the heat of the controversy over the Kennedy Land Trust Bill, the *Grapevine* was founded—a paper representing the interests of island developers and realtors who were opposed to the Kennedy proposal, which, they feared, would put them out of business.

After they took over the other newspapers, the Houghs soon realized they would need additional employees: a reporter, a printer acquainted with the machinery they planned to buy, a real bookkeeper to keep track of accounts, and an advertising person to save Henry from those exhausting by-bicycle solicitations. But to accommodate all this, they needed a bigger *Gazette* office.

At first they used a rental property on Main Street as an annex to the existing office. In an empty storefront, the Houghs installed a secondhand Linotype, the typesetting machine

A drawing of Betty and Henry Hough outside the *Gazette*'s first South Summer Street office, for a greeting card; art by Hough friend Nick Yellenti. *Courtesy of George A. Hough 3rd*

Betty and Henry outside the first South Summer Street *Gazette* office. *Courtesy of the* Vineyard Gazette

that a printer from George Hough Sr.'s *New Bedford Evening Standard* had helped them to buy. But once the type was set here it had to be lugged across Main Street and up the stairs to the main office where the printing was still done.

Larger quarters were finally found in a former watchmaker's shop on South Summer Street just off Main. (The *Gazette* would not have its own building until more than a decade later.) The contents of the two other offices would fit here, along with the three-ton-plus secondhand press, purchased at the advice, again, from a *New Bedford Evening Standard* machinist. A concrete floor was installed and the arrival of the press was impatiently anticipated.

Finally, one afternoon, the eagerly awaited phone call came: the press was at last in Vineyard Haven. But there was a bit of a problem, Henry heard from the other end of the line. The crate containing the press had gone through the wharf while it was being unloaded. Henry didn't wait to hear any more. He and Betty leaped into their Buick and were off to Vineyard Haven. En route they discussed how much salvaging their costly investment from the bottom of the harbor might cost, and how they could borrow more money to do it.

But when they reached the wharf and nervously climbed out of the car to evaluate the damage, they found that although the press had broken a hole in the wharf timbers, and was stuck there, it had not fallen through. A few days later, it was extricated and installed in its Edgartown home.

Meanwhile, the young couple still needed more help. Once again, George Hough Sr. was ready to lend a hand. On his *New Bedford Evening Standard* staff was the enterprising William Roberts, just four years younger than Henry. Bill had worked as a newsboy and an office boy for George Hough and often discussed his future with him. Bill liked the newspaper trade but wasn't sure whether he wanted to be a reporter or a typographer. Ultimately, he decided in favor of becoming a printer and was just finishing his apprenticeship on the *Standard* when George Hough put down his $5,000 for Henry and Betty's newspaper. After the *Gazette* had been equipped with a Linotype and automated printing press, George Hough asked his twenty-two-year-old protégé if he would like a job on the Vineyard. The idea appealed to him and, in 1922, Bill Roberts arrived, bringing the exuberance of youth, intelligence, dependability, curiosity, and a knowledge of the best and the newest in printing technology. Charles Marchant and Bill Roberts became the *Gazette*'s "black gang," as printers called themselves then.

Also living in New Bedford then was a thirty-year-old erstwhile poet who had written occasionally for the *Standard*. Vineyard-born Joseph Chase Allen left the island when he was in his teens to go whaling out of New Bedford. But he got into a tangle with the ship's captain while he was still on the wharf and never even boarded the vessel. Instead, at twenty, Joe Allen enlisted in the cavalry during U.S. involvement in the Mexican civil war. Before he shipped out, however, he got the mumps, and did a tour of duty with the infantry in

Seattle instead. When the altercation ended, he returned to New Bedford. He worked for the New Bedford Shoe Company, making a boring job fun by writing lighthearted jingles on shoeboxes about his fellow workers. His poetizing delighted his co-workers and earned him acclaim.

At his next job, in New Bedford's Weeden Toy Manufacturing Company, the rhythm of the machinery at night set his mind again to the rhythms of verse. One night, on his way home from work, he dropped one of his poems, written on wrapping paper and unsigned, into the *New Bedford Evening Standard* mailbox. The newspaper printed the unknown poet's work; George Hough Sr. searched him out and invited him to write for the paper. When Henry and Betty needed a reporter at the *Gazette,* George Sr., impressed with his writing, recommended Joe. So thirty-year-old Joe Allen joined the *Vineyard Gazette* staff in 1925 and eventually became the public's most beloved *Gazette* writer, producing a folksy weekly column. He titled it "With the Fishermen" and called himself the Wheelhouse Loafer. He drew upon the many hours he spent in the wheelhouses of island tugboats and draggers and in the fishing shacks of Menemsha. He became not only the Vineyard *Gazette*'s mainstay reporter—its "representative-at-large" as he was listed on the masthead—but also its principal ad gatherer. He was loquacious, productive, and kindly.

Soon another printer, Everett Gale from western Massachusetts, joined the staff. Bill Roberts married and brought his wife, Marion, into the *Gazette* family as part-time bookkeeper. "This was how the close-knit crew of the *Gazette* came to be assembled," Hough recalled sixty years later, "and to stick together in labor and companionship through long decades that . . . because of this companionship, seemed to have passed quickly and lightly."

The *Gazette* now had its staff and its equipment, but still needed a permanent home and cash to pay the bills. To earn extra money, in 1923 Henry and Betty left the paper in the hands of their new associates and returned to New York City. Henry took a job doing public relations for the Western Electric Company; Betty became assistant editor of the *Public Health Nurse.* As students, they had enjoyed New York, but working in the city was somehow different—especially after the Vineyard's freedom and fresh air.

"I learned the ups and downs of elevators, morning, noon and night, and in between buses, subways, the tired reek that did for air, and great offices filled with men and women working at desks in an ordered progression that might bring them promotion and might not," Henry recalled.

The young Houghs got cut-rate tickets to the theater, and went frequently, but little else seemed appealing this time in the big city. "It was like Chicago again, but worse," Henry Hough wrote. It was three years before they finally thought they had enough for their newspaper's coffers and happily returned to their $12.50 a week income from the *Gazette.* They were back on the Vineyard again in the spring, just in time to see the apple trees blooming.

Chapter 9

House, Garden, and Meadow

Eight years after their arrival in Edgartown and purchase of the *Gazette,* Henry and Betty Hough decided it was time to have a house as well as a paper of their own. Betty found the site, a pretty piece of pastureland on a quiet dirt road grandiloquently named Pierce Avenue. It was barely a five-minute walk from both the *Gazette* office and the big white whaling mansions above the harbor. Yet just beyond it, fields sloped down to where Sheriff's Meadow Pond gleamed in the sun. There, Louis H. Pease cut ice in winter and, after his death, his daughter Grace Ward continued the ice-cutting business for a time.

Beyond the pond, long-legged herons and silver-white egrets and sometimes a sleek otter fished in the tidal pool called John Butler's Mud Hole. Beyond the mud hole stretched the much larger Eel Pond, and the beach and Nantucket Sound.

The young couple built their house in Colonial style, and painted it white with green shutters. They had it set crosswise on the land rather than parallel to the road, so as many windows as possible would face due south for winter sunshine. The rear view was of the pond and the sound. Inside, to the left of the central hall—ideal for piling books and papers in—was a living room with a fireplace and two walls they soon filled with books. To the right of the hall were the dining room and kitchen.

At the top of the stairs, Henry used the hallway that looked out over the pond as his study, and there were three bedrooms—two with fireplaces—and two baths.

But far more important to them than the house was the garden. At Betty's childhood home in Uniontown grew pink lilies of the valley; even before the new house's foundation was dug, she had asked an aunt in Pennsylvania to send her some. They planted them under a maple tree at what was to be the west side of their house. They also planted

The Colonial-style house the Houghs built was just a five-minute bicycle ride from the *Gazette* office. *Photograph by Joe Munroe, courtesy of the* Vineyard Gazette

hollyhocks and a delphinium (which did not survive). Then Betty, the tree lover, wanted a few dogwoods and a red maple. They also planted lindens and a white fringe tree. A mulberry tree was already on the property, part of a former farm, planted when the farmer had hoped to raise silkworms.

Finally, Betty wanted elms. "I don't think people should stop planting elms," she said, "Dutch elm disease notwithstanding." Once when she was away on a trip to the mainland, Henry planted two six-foot elms to the east of the house. Along with the roses, they grew to become the highlight of the garden. The red-brown flower clusters hanging from their bare limbs were always the first sign of spring. Twice in storms (one of them the hurricane of September 1954) the elms began to lean; a volunteer crew from the *Gazette* office straightened them with a car and a length of sturdy rope.

Roses, like elms, were much beloved by Betty, and, over the years, she inveigled Henry into planting some two hundred varieties of them—hybrid teas, hybrid perpetuals, and climbers. Copper Glow was a particular favorite. Roses lined the path from the front gate to the front door and enveloped the yard in their fragrance. The Vineyard was remarkable for roses, Henry always maintained, since not only was the soil perfect for them, but also the cool summer nights assured a fine color.

A small vegetable garden was just inside the fence, with lettuce and cucumbers, tomatoes and muskmelons. Bird lovers both, they also set up feeders everywhere.

In the backyard was a weather station. Ever since his *New Bedford Evening Standard* summer when he had directed the janitor about which weather flag to fly, Henry had been enamored of weather reporting, and so was Betty. She asked the National Weather Service if she could be one of the 7,000 volunteers who reported findings daily to their headquarters in Asheville, North Carolina, and in 1946 the Weather Service installed a station for them. Early in the morning each press day, either Henry or Betty would check the two thermometers that recorded the maximum and minimum temperatures of the preceding day. They would measure any rain or snowfall and hurry into the office to set the information into type before the *Gazette* went to press. The weather report was considered as important as overnight deaths and accident reports.

For the Houghs' modest income in the 1920s, building their house was an extravagance, so they planned to rent it out during the summers and move to North Tisbury. George Hough Sr. always had his eye out for available land and houses near Fish Hook, and noticed when the old George H. Rogers house came on the market. Betty asked her brother Eleazer, who was doing well with his medical practice, to help her to buy it. For Henry, the house was full of memories of boyhood days munching Mrs. Rogers's sugar cookies and listening to Mr. Rogers's spirited whaling tales, bedazzled by his gold loop earrings. The Rogers house was the perfect place for Henry and Betty to spend their summers—even though it meant a twelve-mile trip back and forth to the *Gazette*.

But the Depression followed quickly on the building of the Houghs' Edgartown house, and they were able to rent it for only one summer. However, they kept the house in North Tisbury as a weekend getaway. Henry's young nephews, George 3d and John, who spent summers with their grandparents at Fish Hook, had gleefully named a little vernal pool in the woods near the Rogers house Lake Elizabeth after Betty. It wasn't the prettiest of ponds, but she accepted the boys' honor with good grace. Here the boys fished assiduously for whales, and Henry planted hybrid blueberries along its bank. In wet years, when this pool stayed full of water into the summer, beautiful water lilies bloomed here. When the Houghs first came in spring to see how the daffodils, myrtle, and lilacs were doing, they sometimes found a Canada goose family swimming there. In fall, when the Indian Hill woods glowed with color, Betty raked up the fallen leaves while Henry planted crocuses. In a rare moment of fantasy in the 1970s, he wrote about the crocuses he loved to ten-year-old Amy Stewart of Chappaquiddick:

"Crocuses are blooming. I do not mean in my yard. My rabbits have such a taste for crocuses that they never have a chance to bloom. But I suppose that yellow and purple crocus flowers look extremely attractive in the rabbit burrows where no doubt they are attractively arranged in vases with the water emptied and renewed each day. I understand that rabbits are good housekeepers but I never knew until a year or so ago that they are artistic. Did you know that?"

Every so often, Henry wrote proper articles on gardening for this magazine or that. Reflecting on his own experience, he commented in one such piece: "The home gardener knows he's pursuing a will-o-the-wisp, yet he plans and works and dreams. If it isn't the thrips which devour his roses, briars and all, it is the Hessian fly. If the cutworms and rabbits don't ruin his dahlias and zinnias, the ear-wigs that crawl by night will see to it. Still, the home gardener labors and dreams." In Henry's case, sometimes the dreams became reality—as when he planted camellias in Edgartown and, rather to the surprise of the American Camellia Society, they grew. Both Houghs were members of the Martha's Vineyard Garden Club, an activist organization promoting the preservation of the island, and Betty was on its board.

At the end of a long summer week, when the *Gazette* finally had been put to bed, the Houghs particularly enjoyed sitting in their garden under the lacy foliage of their elms, and the catbirds "being impatient," Henry wrote, would "descend and light on our shoulders or chairs, and we would get raisins from the kitchen for them or we would have remembered to have a handful of raisins ready for them."

In fall, gleaming goldfinches and chirping chewinks visited their feeders, and pheasants perched on the stone wall behind the house; one took up residence in their broom bush. On winter mornings, the songs of cardinals and the cooing of mourning doves would awaken them. Betty's interest in the birds drawn to their garden inspired her own bird column, "With Avian Visitors." "I make no claims to any success at identification in the field," she wrote. "I am a window watcher, and what passes before that window is rare and strange and wonderful to me. . . . I feel like moving permanently into the kitchen and maintaining a watch through all the daylight hours. . . . Most of my birds are glad to see me again in spring and talk back to me when I address them in baby talk, a most distressing habit. But they are so small and I am so big, the temptation is hard to resist. They seem glad to get home from their southern vacations and we greet them with a big spread since calling out the band or raising the flag might frighten them away."

In their more prosperous years, when Henry and Betty gave occasional summer cocktail parties, they were generally held in this shaded garden full of birds and flowers. Only in the very beginning, however, were the grounds of the Hough house neat and orderly.

That didn't bother either of them. Henry said that he had started out striving for neatness, but his interest was much more in helping things grow than in cutting and pruning them.

"I remember once when I thought things were pretty well kept up, a man leaned over the front fence and remarked, 'This must have been a beautiful place once.' . . . Another observer said our place had a 'Southern look.' I liked that, and so did Betty . . . the instigator of all the planting."

Inside the house, newspapers were stacked everywhere and visitors had to take care not to stumble over them. And there was likely to be collie fur wherever a guest chose to sit. A succession of dogs, principally collies—Rikki-tikki-tavi, Captain Matrix, Dundee Bold, Lochinvar, and, after Betty's death, Graham and Killikrankie, substituted for the children Henry and Betty decided early in their marriage that they did not wish to have. And it was not his philosophy, Henry said, "to live in a house in which a dog could not lie down on the couch in the living room."

The decision not to have a family was based partly on the fear that their limited income from the *Gazette* meant they were not financially stable enough to afford children. And, dedicated as they were to the paper, would they have the time to devote to children? Then Betty, although the daughter and the sister of doctors, had a near phobia about blood. In addition, Henry said he never felt he would have made a good father.

Although Betty would mother the young reporters the *Gazette* acquired, there was nothing of the homemaker about her. A cleaning woman came in weekly and Betty was not inclined to use the kitchen much. At the end of a long day at the office, the prospect of eating out—however simply—appealed to both the Houghs. Their lunches, which they hurried home to eat when the office closed for an hour at noon, tended to be put together with as little effort as possible: sardine sandwiches in summer, more filling fare in winter, such as a liquid bread soup or pea soup perhaps with gingerbread upside-down cake and apples for dessert. On the rare occasions when there were guests besides Henry's family, the housekeeper was pressed into service to cook, too.

But Betty was proud of her ability to prepare a Chicken Casserole Bourgoise, as she called it, from a recipe she had found in *Gourmet* and Henry was proud of his to prepare his mother's chicken chowder. Indeed, he offered it as his example of good, old-fashioned Vineyard cooking to Louise Tate King and Jean Stewart Wexler in 1971 when they compiled *The Martha's Vineyard Cookbook*. And, seafood lovers that they were, the Houghs might serve guests fried scallops since they were easy to prepare, or waffles with clams the housekeeper had stuffed.

When they did eat at home alone, waffles and pancakes were on their supper menu almost as often as sardine sandwiches were for lunch. Sometimes bacon and blue cheese went along with the pancakes; Henry did the cooking. Or he might open a can of beans to serve, cold, with the pancakes.

After supper, they read or, on weekends, Henry and Betty might go to a movie. Neither one of them ever tired of reading or movies. If the night were pleasant, they would stroll with their dog to the town dock to watch the moon on the water. All this would help to calm down newspaper-frazzled nerves.

The couple frequently spent Sundays with Henry's father, taking him and any house-guests for a chicken or lobster dinner at Sally Jeffers' Chappaquiddick Outlook. Mrs. Jeffers was an African-American renowned for her cooking. Afterwards, they might drive down to the gold sand dunes of Wasque and watch the waves roll in at what Henry called "land's end."

Sometimes on weekends they ate out with Edgartown friends at Captain Brown's— occasionally with considerable hilarity. Henry Hough recalled the night they found there was no corkscrew in the restaurant after one member of their party had gone out and bought two bottles of wine. All the restaurant could supply was a cleaver with which they managed to cut off the bottlenecks so neatly that the corks could be reinserted.

At birthday parties Mary Bell Clark Hotchkiss played her piano accordion "looking like some kind of green-clad gnome with a green peaked hat and a feather," Henry remembered, "and trying to get us all to join in singing the chorus of a song ending 'You can't feel blue on the old Red Sea.'"

They also visited the Flynn farmhouse at Pohogonot on Oyster Pond in Edgartown where the Hough family had picnicked with the Flynn family twenty years earlier, Henry and George happily playing with their near contemporaries Tom and George Flynn.

"Much dreaded," Betty wrote of one such dinner party, "but it proved to be extremely pleasant except that I got a headache, probably due to three Manhattans quickly drunk, but partly from laughter, mostly at Tom. Really wonderfully funny." A decade later, Henry and Tom would collaborate when Tom asked Henry to write *An Alcoholic to His Sons*.

"We are butterflying too much," a happy but exhausted Betty wrote about their social whirl.

Then, suddenly, the Houghs' happiness was threatened, in particular the tranquility they enjoyed on Sheriff's Meadow Pond. Widowed Grace Ward, who owned the land around the pond, was growing old. For years the Houghs had watched her in her brown ski suit with its orange collar joining the men when the ice was thick enough to cut, jabbing at it with a pike, and then helping store it in the ice house. The cutting was likely to be early in the morning when the countryside was beautiful with snow patterned with wheel tracks and footprints and sometimes blown into miniature dunes by the wind.

But by the 1950s most homes had electric refrigerators. The last time the ice had been cut was in the previous decade, when during a February thaw Mrs. Ward frantically called in townspeople to cut the ice at night under floodlights before it melted. Not long after that, she had the ice house torn down.

Sheriff's Meadow Pond, where ice was harvested, was just beyond the Hough house.
Photograph by Mark Alan Lovewell

"We were sorry to see the old ice house come down," Hough wrote, "for we never considered it an obstruction of view as some did. It was part of the view. . . ." Every morning, Henry Hough had walked past it with one of his collies. "I walk," he wrote, "to a chorus of red-winged blackbirds, chickadees, robins and mourning doves. We also have a flock of black-crowned night herons, better known as quawks, making their home in the pines. I think the great need is to preserve the whole region from intrusion, and if this can be done, the birds will flock there and multiply."

Only a few years later, Mrs. Ward decided to sell the property around the pond. Development seemed the likely result, which would mean no more walks with dogs through the bittersweet and the yarrow, or redwings in the wild cherries. The muskrats and otters and black-crowned night herons would go as the dwellings and people came. And so one sunny afternoon while Henry Hough nervously worked in the garden, Betty Hough called on Grace Ward. Her mission was to talk her into selling the ten-acre property to her neighbors the Houghs instead of to a developer. However, they had little to offer for it—only $7,500.

The afternoon seemed to stretch on endlessly as Henry nourished and pruned his roses, waiting for Betty. Finally, she returned, full of gaiety. She and Grace had quickly finished their real estate negotiations and had a fine time exchanging Edgartown gossip!

A few years later, after Henry had published the adventure story *Great Days of Whaling* and an agent predicted a great future for him in children's books, Henry and Betty were emboldened to borrow $7,000 to buy five more acres of the Sheriff's Meadow estate abutting the pond. But they felt no need to own it. Taxes on their house were already high and their joint *Gazette* income was still only $16,000. What they wanted, they said, was to have the land and its waters preserved for future generations. (Critics, however, snapped then, and long afterward, that they were simply trying to save it for themselves.) The Houghs asked the Massachusetts Audubon Society about acquiring the ten acres as a sanctuary, but Audubon officials deemed the property too small to be of value to them. Other conservation groups were approached and made the same reply.

And so it was that in 1959, Henry and Betty Hough established the Sheriff's Meadow Foundation "to preserve, administer and maintain natural habitats for wildlife on Martha's Vineyard for educational purposes and in the interest of conservation: to acquire, receive and protect such natural areas so that they may serve as living museums and as a means of assuring to future generations a knowledge of the natural environment of the Island." The conservation movement on Martha's Vineyard had begun—along with antagonism to it.

Chapter 10

Fire!

<u>D</u>ealing with the machinery of the *Gazette,* Henry Hough found himself thoroughly engaged by it. It was the Linotype, in particular, that fascinated him. For efficiency's sake, when there was a late-breaking story—and because there had been only one typewriter in his and Betty's earliest *Gazette* days—he had learned to operate the Linotype. (Betty had, too, but with less enthusiasm.) Henry loved the way a Linotype generated column after column of gleaming fresh type for him. His words flew directly from his fingers to the printing press, through the Linotype's searing hot crucible of liquid lead. After the paper was printed, the metal of the set type was melted down and recycled.

The Linotype wasn't easy to use. It was a big, black, cantankerous, dangerous, and unforgiving machine, but it was the means of transforming the *Gazette* from an obscure nineteenth-century country journal into a modern newspaper—albeit still concerned with the country and old-fashioned values. Henry even liked Linotypes enough to name their third dog, an imposing collie, Matrix, after the Linotype's matrix—the small engraved brass mold from which the letters were cast. Bill Roberts even crafted a weathervane for the *Gazette* that was a giant matrix.

Henry was seldom more contented than when he was in the back shop at work at the Linotype, listening to its clatter, watching the movement of its arm, and knowing that the words he wrote, as soon as he had written them, were ready to be disseminated to readers. There was something "alive" about the process, he said. At a city newspaper, of course, the printers' union would have made the back-shop Linotype off-limits to him as management; here it wasn't.

Henry had carefully watched, and tried to assist, in the assembling of the first Linotype he and Betty had bought—one of the first made by the company that invented them, founded in the 1890s. He recognized that he had no aptitude for mechanics. (In her diary, Betty remembered, with mixed amusement and frustration, the January night when the furnace pipe slipped and Henry tried to fix it. A piece fell out. "There were tantrums on both sides. I rushed off in the car to Bill's to get him to go over and try to bring Henry to his senses.") But Henry found himself responsible, once the Linotype was in place, for keeping it in working order. After laboring to get it going again after it had angrily spewed forth matrices once, he described it as a mechanical adolescent—independent and often hostile, he said. Nonetheless it produced his copy. He began to speculate, however, about how much better a typesetting machine that worked more like a typewriter would be for a small newspaper than a Linotype. He envisioned a machine that was simple and manageable, that set the type directly without all the mechanical folderol of the Linotype.

Henry wrote with as much ease on a Linotype machine as on a typewriter.
Photograph by Gretchen Van Tassel, courtesy of the Vineyard Gazette

Henry decided to invent it himself. When his invention was ready, he consulted a patent attorney in Boston and, in 1931, he became the proud recipient of a patent.

But then there was the matter of marketing. Filled with enthusiasm, Henry went on one of his rare trips off-island to describe his invention to a New York newspaper editor who had also devised a modification of the Linotype. Hough explained that what was important about his machine was that the type was set by the writer, without a middleman compositor. The city newspaper editor was silent for a moment, then gruffly pointed out to the country editor that things weren't done that way in a proper newspaper office: copy went from a reporter's typewriter to a copy desk to a composing room. Although he thought Henry's invention probably would work, the editor said he didn't think any printing company would buy and manufacture it.

His enthusiasm only slightly subdued, Henry went with his plans to two factories producing printing machines. At one, he was brusquely told that the Linotype, as it was, was perfectly satisfactory and nothing else was needed. At the other, they said that photo-composition was on the way, and that was all that interested them. His final visit was to the successful inventor of a stereotyping process newspapers had begun to use. There the advice was simple and straightforward: the quality and ingenuity of his invention didn't matter, he was informed. Marketing an invention brought nothing but sorrow. He would be a happier man if he simply threw his patent into Vineyard Sound before it ruined his life.

The young editor's exuberance diminished and he returned gloomily to the Vineyard. His invention never was produced, and he and Betty used the drawing he had had done for the patent application as their Christmas card.

Another and ultimately more profitable venture of the 1930s was Henry's first book. Originating as a series of *Gazette* articles, the book traced the Vineyard's history as a summer resort. Henry began with Bartholomew Gosnold's visit in 1620, and wrote of Nathaniel Hawthorne on the island in 1870 and of President Grant and his wife's visit in 1876. The heavy-drinking president was so moved by the hallelujahs, amens, and singing at a Camp Meeting service in Cottage City that a pastor believed the President found peace with God then and there, Hough reported in *Martha's Vineyard: Summer Resort, 1835–1935*.

He also wrote of the land companies buying up Vineyard property in the second half of the nineteenth century (a harbinger of things to come). They bought land on the bluffs above the Lagoon, on the seemingly endless expanse of Katama outside Edgartown, among the red cedar trees of West Chop. He wrote of the grand hotels with wraparound porches, and of the construction of bathing pavilions.

Henry sent the finished manuscript to a publisher with the same enthusiasm he had exhibited when he tackled New York with his printing machine. Until near the end of his life, Henry Hough's optimistic vitality was evident in the pace of his steps on a walk, the speed of his writing (even though he never learned to type with more than two fingers), and his conviction, like his father's, that right would conquer might. But he had no more luck selling his first book than his invention. The publisher responded that it was too detailed to appeal to an audience beyond the Vineyard.

Publishing a book, however, was easier to do on one's own than producing a printing machine. Henry and Betty agreed that he should borrow enough money to have an edition of 2,000 printed. Although Henry neither made nor lost money from it, *Martha's Vineyard: Summer Resort* did attract national attention. He sent out review copies, and a *New York Times* column about the book called it "important local history." The reviewer noted that, though its subject was an island of only one hundred square miles, the book deserved the attention of anyone interested in understanding nineteenth-century America.

Over the years, Henry Hough would write twenty-six more books, with many favorable reviews, but that first one gave him infinite pleasure. He had become a writer at last. With determination, endless energy, a head always bursting with ideas, and Betty's constant encouragement, he would write more history, as well as novels, children's books, essays, short stories, and memoirs. Eventually, as he had long hoped, the writing of books occupied most of his time; increasingly, he would leave the newspaper to Betty. Even when he was the one heralded for the paper, he never failed to give her credit both for the *Gazette*'s and for his own success.

"She played the decisive part in the *Gazette*," he said. "Her influence can be sharply defined. . . . In the long, lean years before World War II when weeklies got no national advertising, I did a great deal of the typesetting and the chasing of local ads, but it was Betty who held the fort and edited the paper."

As for her influence on his books, Henry dedicated all of his novels to her. So much of what he wrote, according to Henry, was praiseworthy only because Betty had urged him to write it and then made him rewrite and rewrite it.

But in the 1930s Henry still could not commit himself to book writing; the *Gazette* still had a long way to go.

On a rare spring vacation trip to the mainland in 1935, the Houghs were visiting Baltimore when a garbled message arrived that the *Gazette* had burned down. When Henry finally got through to Bill Roberts, he found out that the situation was not quite that bad—though bad enough. Bill urged him to get home as soon as possible. Leaving Betty and their Buick behind, Henry took the bus and train, where a fellow passenger, learning that Henry was from the Vineyard, asked if he knew about the fire at the *Vineyard Gazette*. The latest word, its horrified editor-publisher heard, was that it was still burning.

But when Henry finally arrived in Edgartown that night, he found that the building still stood. The fire had started in an electric switch box just at suppertime when everyone had gone home. It had quickly spread to sheathing on the walls, and to newspapers. But there was a hero of the day: twelve-year-old Bobby Morgan, who lived upstairs on the street

Natty Bill Roberts from the *New Bedford Evening Standard* was the *Gazette*'s back-shop foreman. *Photograph by Gretchen Van Tassel, courtesy of the* Vineyard Gazette

behind, was looking out the window from the dinner table and saw a plume of smoke rising from the *Gazette* roof. He told his father, schooner captain Fred B. Morgan, who happened to be at home at the time. Within seconds, the whole family was out on the street alerting neighbors and the fire department. Meanwhile, Horace Vincent, who owned the house next door, trained his garden hose on the flames.

Damage was extensive, but repairs could be made. Volunteers had carried the files to safety and the firemen took great care to avoid water damage whenever possible. The machines, purchased with such deliberation, were soaked, but Bill Roberts had already contacted their manufacturers and their mechanics would take them apart, clean, and reassemble them. Insurance paid for the damage. As for that week's *Gazette,* Henry's brother, George, printed it for him. By that time, George had become a country newspaper editor, too. He was editor and publisher of the *Falmouth Enterprise,* just over the water on Cape Cod.

Order was restored as much as it could be. City-born Henry, musing on the long bus and train trip back to Baltimore to retrieve Betty, likened the generosity and friendship of small-town people in an emergency to an extended family.

When he and Betty were home again, they made sure that a baseball glove, ball, and bat were set aside at Hall's Department Store for young Bobby Morgan. The boy couldn't have been more pleased when the store owner called him inside from the street and presented him with his three rewards. In later years, Bob Morgan was a county official who frequently disagreed with the Houghs' stands in their newspaper, but he never forgot their thoughtful gifts.

At the time of the fire, the *Gazette* had been in the old watch repair shop shaped like a bowling alley for nearly two decades. Henry and Betty viewed the place with a certain affection. "We liked the gentle ruin which wear and tear had produced, the jumble, the

The bridge at the Old Ford in North Tisbury. *Photograph by E. Malcolm Phillips, courtesy of the* Vineyard Gazette

honored as its Man of the Year. Little did he know, in the 1920s, how often in the years ahead he would oppose road construction and the policies of the boat company serving the island. Although Henry often found support for conservation among the summer people, eventually their numbers and new home construction would become the greatest threats to the little island whose woods and dunes and moors he and Betty strove to preserve. "The *Gazette*," he admitted in 1975, looking back, "was soon advocating a program of advancement for Martha's Vineyard which in today's context might be alarming . . . but I do not think it nearly as bad as it might have been."

Eleven years into their editorship, the Houghs and the Martha's Vineyard Garden Club, then seven years old, were confronted with the first of many road "improvements" they could not endorse. In Henry's childhood he had often seen the mail stage come in to the North Tisbury post office from Vineyard Haven; then the post horses cooled off at the

Mill River ford. "Here, the swamp maples hang out banners in fall," was how Henry Hough described it, "and the brook ripples and leaps over stones and past the informal line of native shrubs. Here a segment of natural beauty and old times is opened to the observation of all passers who have quick eyes and hearts."

But the Massachusetts Highway Commission didn't see it that way in 1931. The State Artery rules were to eliminate curves and fell any trees in the way. The state officials were close to making the North Tisbury road at the ford almost unrecognizable when the Garden Club and the *Gazette* led public opinion against the project; the Highway Commission agreed that on little Martha's Vineyard state regulations need not apply.

Twenty years later, however, the state again planned to widen the road, to create a thoroughfare suitable for sightseer tour buses and for automobile drivers who did not like curves. The state Department of Public Works announced it would add nine and a half feet in width to the approach to the ford and would be cutting down eighteen trees to do it. Henry Hough's plan of improving travel to and on the Vineyard to bring more tourists was going awry.

In the pages of the *Gazette*, he pointed out that more than just the ford was at stake. The effort to widen the bridge unnecessarily and straighten a winding road was simply a symbol of all such attacks on the island's scenic values. Mainland highway standards should bear no relation to a twenty-mile-long island whose great wealth was its unspoiled natural beauty, he wrote. And the Garden Club president exclaimed that "if the assets of the Island are lost and the reasons why people come here from the four corners of the earth to visit are eliminated, everyone will lose out."

Seasonal visitors from as far away as Cincinnati, urged on by the *Gazette*, decried the need for "mainland standardization" on the rural Vineyard. One irate protestor, writing directly to the Department of Public Works, complained that "you men in Boston . . . will not take it that we on the Island are a set apart community." His suggestion: "Go to another community to spend the state money. For we do not want you to spend it here."

A New Jersey woman opposed to the widening feared that the state was seeking to create speedways on the Vineyard and that reckless driving would ensue. In the end, after several months, Commissioner of Public Works William F. Callahan good-naturedly gave in to the *Gazette* and its readers. He remarked that his project had been done in by island socialites and he was off to Florida to recuperate from "having run up a white flag of surrender. The cause of conservation has been victorious again."

But it wasn't always. A few years later oak-shaded Middle Road, edged by wild rose hedgerows and stone walls, was threatened with leveling and widening. Up hill and down dale the Middle Road winds through the farming communities of West Tisbury and Chilmark. But after an automobile accident on the road's Chilmark segment, town fathers were criticized for inadequate upkeep. They turned to the state for help. It was readily provided, but along with state money, voters feared, would come that inevitable widening to meet Commonwealth standards. The walls bordering old fields would be endangered.

A *Gazette* correspondent poetized:

> Oh, leave the Middle Road alone!
> And let it wind between its walls
> Of tumbled, vine-clad mossy stone,
> Beneath the shade of twisted oaks,
> Between the hedgerows green and straight.

Henry was also quick to come to the old road's defense. He wrote about how it mounts "among great shapely hills beside long gray ribbons of stone walls and dips into woody valleys." He wrote of the vistas of the blue-green ocean from it. And he told of how the road went by the hill where the town hall once had stood, known, in disparaging Vineyard fashion, as Woodpecker Hall.

"The defenders of the Middle Road are rallying, and we hope their strength may be as the multitudes. Long ago the road was improved so that it could be traversed in winter and in all sorts of weather. What more can anyone desire? . . . Further development of this last remaining country highway would surely yield not more but less. Carried beyond its present point, 'development' and 'improvement' would involve destruction of the character Islanders so much love, the loss of natural resources and the standardization of a strongly individual road into an imitation of countless thousands on the mainland."

He was having second thoughts about road improvement, but his editorial went on to reflect the interest he still had in furthering the island's economy: "Here again there is no conflict between sentiment and business judgment. Sound business and sentiment are on the same side. The preservation of the road, its bordering hedgerows and walls, its overhanging limbs, its vistas of rolling countryside, is a matter of dollars and cents. Visitors come to the Vineyard for just such enjoyments as this noble old road offers."

The following summer, all but two property owners along the road petitioned the state to respect the Middle Road's scenic quality. By now, Henry Hough had begun to develop the political skills that—until the failure of the Kennedy Bill at the end of his life—would prove so important in his efforts to preserve the Vineyard. He remembered Pen Dudley's Chicago lessons on the value of seeing an opponent's viewpoint and of sometimes being conciliatory. He included in his editorial supporting the Middle Road petitioners this nod to the state: "No one for a moment believes that the commissioner, or any other state authority, would willingly oppose the wishes of the island in this matter, or sacrifice the values which the Middle Road embraces. The danger is that the road may be modernized simply as a routine matter."

A spokesman for the Department of Public Works then soothingly replied that even though vegetation had been disturbed by the construction, he was sure that, graded and seeded, the roadside would look much as it had before. "I can assure you that it is the desire of the department to in no way disturb the beauties of our roadsides."

That didn't quite happen, but without local and *Gazette* protest it could have been worse. The Middle Road was widened and leveled so that stone walls that had once been high enough to keep cattle inside them were, now, with the raised roadbed, low enough for the animals to simply step across. The roadsides were seeded, but bayberries, blueberries, and huckleberries were uprooted by workmen's tractors. Only the diligence of Chilmark hairdresser Rena Fischer, looking out her window as a road worker readied to chop down a historic beetlebung tree, saved it from destruction.

While the Old Ford and the Middle Road controversies were going on in North Tisbury and Chilmark, Henry and Betty Hough were also keeping an eye on events in Edgartown that threatened the uniqueness of its environment.

The white wooden Edgartown Lighthouse was in disrepair. In 1939, it was more than a hundred years old and had suffered considerably in the hurricane of the preceding year. The Lighthouse Service decided to replace it with a state-of-the-art steel skeleton structure and an automatic light. But all Edgartown—with the "aggressive and accomplished editor" of the *Vineyard Gazette* in the forefront, as reported—"was up in arms." Every week the *Gazette* devoted columns to long editorials "of fiery eloquence," it added.

The idea of a bare steel structure at the entrance to the historic harbor where whaleships once had moored was outrageous. To emphasize this, copies of the *Vineyard Gazette* marked to show references to the demolition plan were sent to the Commissioner of Lighthouses and the state Secretary of Commerce every week. A town meeting was called so the commissioner could explain his stand to all townspeople and, above all, to Henry Hough, who by now was "the recognized leader of the protest parade." Henry and those he had stirred to action prevailed. The Commissioner of Lighthouses finally agreed to move a traditional conical-shaped, cast-iron lighthouse from an isolated Ipswich, Massachusetts, site to Edgartown harbor.

Henry and Betty were delighted at this victory, yet increasingly dismayed at the results of the economic prosperity they had promoted. Both the year-round population and, more substantially, the number of summer visitors to the Vineyard were rising, along with their cars. In 1927, the *Gazette* had applauded the resurfacing of the state road from Vineyard Haven to Edgartown but, by 1969, when federal as well as state monies were received to widen it for traffic, Henry was writing of the "utter devastation" by work crews to that same back road.

"The destruction of trees is appalling, and this, with the ravaging of the roadsides and savage substitution of engineering geometry for all that was natural and appropriate, is to result in the kind of highway Martha's Vineyard does not need and does not want.

"If the lesson was not clear before, it is painfully clear now; to exchange the independence of Island towns and their control over their own affairs for allotments of federal and state money comes down at the last to one of the worst bargains of the modern world. Old landmarks disappear before the bulldozer and with them goes something important to our way of life."

In 1946 the Houghs launched another preservation campaign. The seventeenth-century John Coffin property on North Water Street was to be sold at auction, then probably torn down and the land divided into cheap shops, alleys, and parking lots.

A friend suggested that a corporation be formed to acquire the property and adapt it for some suitable purpose that would pay for itself. To start the project off, Henry and Betty put up $1,000. A few years later, they had the satisfaction of reporting in the *Gazette* that the building was preserved as apartments and an antiques store, which provided income to reimburse the original members of the North Water Street Corporation.

"Edgartown," Henry Hough had written in those early years, "is different even from other towns on Martha's Vineyard. . . . It is at the end of the road, so there is no through traffic. It has stood from the beginning between the land and the sea, combining the flavor of one with the elemental usefulness of the other. . . . Edgartown is a kind of solitary outpost where the greatest product, peace of mind, is free to all." He and Betty were to spend their lives seeking to keep it that way.

Chapter 12

Murder at East Chop

The Houghs' limited income (Henry and Betty put any extra money they earned back into the *Gazette)* and the endless hours at the office constrained the couple's vacation possibilities, along with Henry's firm conviction that the best place to be was home. However, particularly in the '30s and early '40s, the Houghs managed a few trips off-island, including one to Betty's friends in Baltimore (interrupted by the *Gazette* fire) and two visits to Pennsylvania so Betty could show Henry the beloved mountains of her childhood.

In Betty's birthplace of Uniontown, Henry found strange parallels with New Bedford. Once Uniontown had been a farming and trading community, as New Bedford had been a whaling center. Then coal was discovered, and mines ravaged the countryside, coke ovens sprang up everywhere, and industrial smoke enveloped the city. Then, as quickly as it had arrived, the coal industry vanished.

Henry was not taken with the city, finding it depressing and drab. But his sensibility was stirred, like his wife's, by the round hills and sweeping contours beyond the city. When they drove up to Betty's beloved Pine Knob, where she had summered, he found a rich green glade on a craggy mountaintop where they gathered white and yellow violets. Henry had never seen yellow violets before. A wild plum was in full bloom in a field and the chewinks in the trees reminded Henry of the Vineyard.

Here amid Pine Knob's tall trees and fields of wildflowers Betty had ridden her horses and roamed with her collies, as integral a part of her young life as North Tisbury's woods and shores had been of Henry's. Here Betty had fallen from her donkey, Jack, and broken her arm. Even though her arm was never wholly right again, she never held this against Jack or any other living creature; all her life she fought for the rights of animals. In time, when she and her brother Eleazer, a doctor living in New Orleans, realized their visits to Pine

Knob were dwindling, they gave the land to the Pennsylvania State Forest System. But Betty always kept a picture of it tucked into the mirror on her bedroom dresser on the Vineyard.

Other holiday trips took Henry and Betty to Chapel Hill, North Carolina, where they and Louis and Mildred Graves, editors of the *Chapel Hill Weekly,* spent long hours discussing the problems of small-town newspapers. When Henry decided to write a biography of fellow naturalist Henry David Thoreau, they visited Walden Pond in Concord. Henry's talk for the Maine Library Association brought them to Friendship, Maine.

Most often, their trips were to New York. Henry served as a Pulitzer Prize juror three times. A trifle apologetically, he had to explain to Pulitzer committee chairman John Hohenberg that—country editors as they were—he and Betty could not afford to stay at the Waldorf Astoria with most of the other jurors. They found less pricey hotels and thoroughly enjoyed those New York visits, reminiscing about journalism school days, seeing old friends, and going to the theater, a lifelong interest nurtured in his New Bedford childhood and pursued at Columbia and in Washington and Chicago.

As the Vineyard increased in popularity as a summer resort and the *Gazette* grew busier, the Houghs had less and less time for distant off-island vacations, or even for trips to Boston or New York to see a play. They had to be satisfied with films at one of the island's five movie theaters, or shows at its summer playhouse. Fortunately, productions at the Phidelah Rice School of the Spoken Word were of high quality.

The school and its theater were set among pines and scrub oaks at an intersection of sandy roads in the East Chop section of Oak Bluffs. In winter, its owners, Phidelah and Elizabeth Rice, taught theater in Boston and were readers at the First Church of Christ, Scientist; Phidelah had also acted on Broadway. In 1911, with four of their students, the Rices began a summer acting school in the Methodist Camp Ground in Oak Bluffs. Over the years, the school and its performances—the second oldest summer theater in the United States—expanded to a campus of seven buildings, including dormitories, a dining facility, a three-hundred-seat theater, and the smaller Bandbox Theater for matinees. Productions ranged from such light fare as *Bill of Divorcement* and Sir James Barrie's *The Twelve-Pound Look* to Henrik Ibsen's tragic *A Doll's House.*

On early summer evenings at the playhouse, Henry and Betty would walk out to the bluffs at intermission to watch the sun set over the Vineyard and Nantucket sounds. By summer's end, they could "hear the locusts and smell the pines in the full velvet of night itself. The bright stars and the Milky Way were the real proscenium, and if the whistle of the late steamboat could be heard during the action of the play, we did not mind, and for us the illusion was not spoiled," Henry recalled in his 1950 book *Once More the Thunderer.*

They were staunch supporters of the theater, both as patrons and in the pages of the *Gazette.* Plays were always reviewed and interesting actors and actresses were interviewed by the young reporters added to the staff by then. But in June of 1940, everything changed at the Phidelah Rice School of the Spoken Word. Phidelah was not well that summer and leased the theater to Charles Emerson Cook, who arrived with his own troupe of actors and stage crew. Elizabeth Rice continued teaching at the school and Phidelah's younger brother, Ralph Huntingdon Rice, joined the faculty. The younger Rice, despite being enamored of the stage like his brother, was a shy, withdrawn loner.

Then, on the night of June 29, there was a murder at the Phidelah Rice School; Ralph Rice was the prime suspect. Raped and bludgeoned that night was seventy-two-year-old Clara Smith, a Christian Science practitioner training to be a reader. (The school offered instruction in effective pulpit reading from the works of Christian Science founder Mary Baker Eddy.) Mrs. Smith had gone to her dormitory room in Sumner Hall on the East Chop bluffs about 9 p.m. that Saturday. The following morning, when a friend tried to waken her for breakfast, her body was found hidden under the bedclothes. A week and a day later, loner Ralph Rice was arrested and taken to the sprawling white Edgartown jail, charged with the rape and murder of Mrs. Smith. In three hundred years, only two other murders had been committed on Martha's Vineyard.

Before Rice's arrest, two other suspects had been interrogated—a boy who was charged with a minor theft, and Harold Tracy, an electrician with the theater company that had rented the playhouse. A man on parole from a ten-year sentence for car theft in Indiana, and wanted for possible involvement in a Kentucky jewel heist, Tracy was found to be in possession of a gun and was sentenced to a year in the Barnstable House of Correction on Cape Cod for having a concealed weapon.

But it was the slightly "peculiar" Mr. Rice, the district attorney had decided, whom he would put on trial for the murder. Betty, the *Gazette's* longtime principal court reporter, Joe Allen, and, occasionally, Henry covered the trial. Before it was over, the trial had taken up fifty or so columns in two issues of the *Gazette*—"the equivalent of a good-sized novel," Henry later wrote.

Tracy testified briefly as to his whereabouts the night of the crime. The case against Rice was largely based on distraught correspondence during the week of the crime with his Christian Science practitioner in New York. She, too, was called to the stand.

The jury deliberated only one hour and five minutes before finding Ralph Huntingdon Rice not guilty; the Houghs had not thought him guilty either. But then who had killed Clara Smith? Henry and Betty wanted to know.

"The trial had spread upon public record certain evidence that needed more attention than it had yet received," Henry wrote in *Once More the Thunderer*, where he fully recounted the murder and trial (but changed the names of all those involved). "We were afraid the district attorney would drop everything . . . and therefore it was up to the *Gazette* to force the issue, and force it we did. . . . We had no desire to convict Harris," Henry wrote, using this name for Tracy, "but there were 14 points of possible suspicion . . . and no apparent leads in any other direction." These facts included Tracy's attentions to an attractive young actress and his having her dormitory window pointed out to him; later she had exchanged that room with the elderly Mrs. Smith. Also, the night of the murder, Tracy had told his friends that he was going out to get a woman. Later, at the Edgartown jail on the hidden gun charge, he had admitted to the matron that when he woke up from a drunken stupor Sunday morning on the stairs in the dormitory where the murder had occurred, he had no idea how he had gotten there.

In March 1941 Henry sent a letter to the district attorney pointing out that considerable evidence about Tracy and his activities the night of the murder were a matter of public knowledge that should have been put before the grand jury. "This letter is not in any sense intended to dictate or to bring about action opposed to your better judgment. My own attitude and that of the *Gazette* is solely one of cooperation and our desire to send you in the way of aspects of the case which are being strongly considered by the Island public, many of which might not otherwise have come to your attention.

"Of course if you do not feel that the county is justified in spending the money to make a complete investigation to bring the necessary witnesses to testify before the grand jury, I will agree with you that it is better not to do anything at all. To serve the purpose which is so important to the public through solution of a case which remains a blot and a reproach to the Island any investigation must be complete.

"I am writing this now because I know steps must be taken immediately to be successful."

The spring term of superior court was scheduled for April in Edgartown. Henry and Betty were sure that if Tracy's case was not considered then, it never would be. As it turned out, Tracy escaped from the Barnstable House of Correction just before the sitting of the superior court. But all through March, Henry had not only been writing to the district attorney, but also preparing editorials about the murder case. When he and Betty were called before the grand jury, they knew their campaign had been effective.

Getting Tracy back to Edgartown, however, proved difficult. First, he had to serve the rest of his sentence in Indiana, then he was returned to Massachusetts to serve time for breaking out of jail. Not until 1946 did he finally appear before superior court. Briefly, the Houghs rejoiced that their work had borne fruit and Tracy had been indicted. But their joy was short-lived. So much time had elapsed since the murder and so many witnesses had disappeared that the district attorney did not think the evidence warranted a new trial.

"With the freeing of Harold Tracy by the superior court . . . the atrocious Island murder of 1940 slips away into the annals of unsolved crimes. . . . That a costly trial, with all its unfortunate accompaniments, is unnecessary, the Island is doubtless glad, but that the crime remains without solution and without punishment will always be the cause of deep regret," Henry editorialized.

Sometimes country newspaper editors win their fights. Sometimes they don't.

Chapter 13

All Living Creatures

If ever there were kindred spirits, they were Betty and Henry Hough and Katharine M. Foote, the indefatigable five-foot-tall founder and director of the Vineyard's Animal Rescue League. Kitty Foote had first come to the island from Boston as a child in the 1870s, when there were still tents under the great oaks in the Methodist Camp Ground. Then, just as Henry and Betty were settling into the *Gazette*, she had returned to Edgartown to make it her home. By this time, she was a retiree in her sixties. The life she lived from then until her death in 1955 at the age of ninety-three could not have been fuller or richer. This petite defender of animals was often at the *Gazette*, pleading the cause—always successfully—of the animals to which she was so devoted. The difference in her age and the Houghs' didn't matter; what mattered was that both the young editors and the white-haired Bostonian shared a love for all living creatures.

Many *Gazette* readers were openly annoyed at the Houghs' devotion to birds and animals. Others simply found it silly. Readers from off-island metropolitan areas tended to find Henry's and Betty's fixation with birds and dogs, in particular, quaint and amusing. Front-page boxes in the paper seeking homes for abandoned summer pets and headlines announcing "Shipwrecked Cat Finds New Home in Grocery" and "Visiting Pig Trots Away on Its Social Affairs" met with considerable eye-rolling, as did full-length obituaries of pets. Imaginary interviews were conducted by Matrix, or one of his collie successors, with a dog in some dire strait; for example, the first dog sent into space. Come summer, an animal social column by Anon (Betty Hough) often announced the arrival, by name, in Edgartown of longtime canine and feline seasonal visitors.

But without the *Gazette*'s concern for wildlife, indiscriminate DDT spraying in the 1960s and '70s to eliminate gypsy moths would have destroyed the Imperial moths as well. The luna moth found a safe haven in the frost bottoms of the island's state forest, too.

In 1957, when a helicopter released mosquito pesticide over the West Tisbury school grounds just as the children had gone outdoors to eat their lunches, the *Gazette* gave the story prominent play. The paper also reported how arsenate of lead, a powerful chemical hand-sprayed on poison ivy, also killed newly planted grapevines a considerable distance away. The *Gazette* became particularly indignant when the little son of pressman Everett Gale, deciding to "play cow," nibbled on grass that was sprayed and had to be rushed to the hospital. The resulting brouhaha over the spraying of poisons persuaded county officials to call off state-proposed aerial spraying of the Vineyard's freshwater marshes to kill mosquitoes.

In another incident, in 1959, the state Department of Public Works announced it would be applying a soil sterilant along guardrails on the island's state roads to prevent undesirable growth. Henry and Betty were aghast again and Henry editorialized so fiercely

Indomitable Katharine M. Foote, founder and director of the Vineyard's Animal Rescue League, had staunch allies in Henry and Betty Hough. *Courtesy of the* Vineyard Gazette

that, a few days later, the spraying was "postponed." In general, Henry and Betty were opposed to upsetting nature by artificial means.

Sometimes, however, despite their respect for all natural life, the Houghs were hard-pressed to decide whether to protect trees afflicted by predator insects or birds at risk from eating the spray-poisoned bugs. In June of 1954, armies of cankerworms could, it was said, almost be heard munching as they made their way through the oaks, elms, and maples of the Lambert's Cove area of Tisbury and West Tisbury. At Seven Gates Farm, the devastation was so great the woods looked as if a forest fire had blazed through them. Mohu, the Lambert's Cove property of Beatrice Butler, president of the Garden Club and daughter of the senator who acquired so many acres on the North Shore in Henry's childhood, was especially hard hit. She launched an all-out campaign for spraying.

Betty, in her colorful story about it, remarked that "the chomping jaws of the canker-worms . . . are almost frighteningly audible. . . . and their droppings spatter the roads and woods, as well as passersby, sounding like the patter of rain. Although spraying seems the only solution . . . there are those who hesitate to use this defensive measure at this partic-ular time of year," she added, "when the gaping mouths of thousands of baby birds are turned heavenward to receive the manna dropped by their parents, and, in this case, it is feared, the death brought from the sky by the spraying machine." If the worms came to her property—even if her beloved elms were attacked—she would go to the Supreme Court to prevent any poisoning of the air and the birds above her, she said.

The cankerworm battle was also a difficult one for the Houghs because Betty was a board member of the Garden Club which, along with Katharine Foote, had been the Houghs' staunchest ally in the anti-pesticide campaigns.

And then there were the woodticks that caused Rocky Mountain spotted fever in people and tormented pets. A few years after the Houghs had become *Gazette* editors, Betty had covered a Garden Club lecture about releasing parasites that laid eggs in woodtick nymphs and thereby destroyed them. Woodticks were anathema to any collie owner, and this nat-ural means of riddance so intrigued Betty that she began soliciting money for a Martha's Vineyard Woodtick Fund. A June 1936 page-one *Gazette* headline read "Gazette Asks Funds for Woodtick Study to Begin at Once." A Vineyard-visiting Harvard entomologist volun-teered to study the life cycle of the tick on the island and Katharine Foote offered labo-ratory space for the work at her Animal Rescue League. With the money the *Gazette* had collected, the study went on for a year, but more time was needed. The U.S. Department of Agriculture offered help but no money.

As difficult as it was for her to be political, Betty made herself follow the lead of her father-in-law and husband, and asked a congressman—whose campaigns she had covered in her *New Bedford Evening Standard* days—if he could help out. He succeeded in getting the Department of Agriculture to appropriate $10,000 for the study. The woodtick project, the first of its kind in the nation, attracted sufficient attention to be taken over by the federal government, until World War II broke out and the project ended.

In the 1960s, Henry believed government scientists endorsing DDT—despite Rachel Carson's much publicized outcry against it—should consider its effect on island scallops and oysters. "It will be a grim thing if the island discovers too late that the shellfish industry is being halted because of DDT contamination," he wrote.

The protection of wildfowl—ducks, Canada geese, pheasants, and quail—and of rabbits and deer from hunters was also a Hough priority. It was no accident one deer season that a gun advertisement was placed above a No Hunting, No Trespassing advertisement. This prompted perplexed chief ad-gatherer Joe Allen to write to Betty: "Darling Mrs. Hough: Mine is a sad and sordid existence. Between you whose feelings are hurt and the advertiser who thought it was a dirty trick to put his gun ad over the No Trespassing ad . . . What to do, I ask? Thinking about the revenue of the *Gazette*, I try to make peace first with the advertiser. Is that wrong? And now, regardless, he is mad clear through! Lovingly yours, J.C.A."

All Hough property in North Tisbury was posted with No Hunting and No Trapping signs; the otters and muskrats in island ponds needed protection, too. Toward the end of his life, when Hough had sold the *Gazette* but served as its editor, a columnist wrote a piece extolling deer-hunting that Henry, distracted with other matters, almost let slip by him. Had it appeared, an enraged Henry told the columnist, he would have left the paper and never returned. (But in a curious postscript he added, "I might not myself feel so strongly if this were not a matter to which my wife gave her most fiery and unremitting devotion for many, many years!")

Grimly remembering his year with the meatpacking association, Henry strongly endorsed improvement in humane slaughter methods. Slaughterhouse procedures weren't a local subject, but if the Houghs felt strongly about a topic, they sometimes reprinted pieces from off-island papers on such off-island matters in an editorial comment section. With his political skill, Henry sometimes also wrote letters to government officials about their concerns. For example, although he was vehemently against Richard Nixon—remarking when Nixon ran for his second term that he and Betty would be doubling their contributions to the Friends of the Earth and local conservation groups to counteract the Republican president's negative approach to conservation issues—Hough swallowed his pride in 1971 and wrote to Nixon thanking him for helping create the Animal Health Division of the Department of Agriculture: "Nothing that now happens should impair the effectiveness of the agency you have helped so thoughtfully—and so consistently with your love of dogs and other animals—to bring into being. . . . Whatever else may separate the American people, they come together in causes such as this and your leadership is everywhere valued among those who abhor cruelty and cherish mercy and understanding.

I speak as one long involved in the cause of animals who share with us the larger citizenship of the natural world."

After the *Gazette,* most important in Henry and Betty's lives were their collie dogs. From a dog, Henry wrote, one receives loyalty, companionship, humor, the care of a guardian, and youth. The whole exuberant nature of a dog persuades one to be young, he felt. Thus for years the *Gazette* without a wagging tail greeting visitors at the door would have been unthinkable.

Captain Matrix (during the war he acquired his military title) died in 1949 at the age of twelve. In his last years, his hind legs were paralyzed and his owners were often criticized for keeping him alive longer than many people felt appropriate. Henry had rigged up a wheelbarrow-like carrier to hold the legs, so he could continue to take Matsy (Matrix's nickname) on walks. A black-bordered reproduction of a painting of him by Diana Mcilvaine, entitled "Captain Matrix, A Member of Our Staff," filled the lead editorial space of October 28, 1949. "Matrix worked at the *Gazette* as we did," heartbroken Henry wrote, "and was indignant or forlorn on the infrequent occasions when he was prevented from going to the office in business hours."

Dundee Bold came next in 1950. He is remembered in *Gazette* columns by the headline "Dundee Is Collecting Mementoes of the Past" when he dug up arrowheads in the *Gazette* yard, and for the time his "guardian" (Betty) was pulled to her knees by him as they crossed North Water Street and were attacked by a pack of dogs. His seventh birthday party was also a headlined event. Betty and Henry hurried home from an off-island vacation to present him with, among other gifts, a vanilla ice cream cone.

Lochinvar was Dundee's successor, selected by Betty from some sixty puppies at a show in Framingham, Massachusetts. He was notable for a fight with the dog of local doctor Robert Nevin. The dogs met head on during a walk in Sheriff's Meadow and, Henry admitted, Lochie went after the doctor's Labrador retriever. Henry added, "Obviously, he had no choice. He didn't want any other male dog anywhere in the Sheriff's Meadow protectorate." No veterinarian was on the island, so the country editor and the country doctor hurried back to the doctor's office where Henry held Lochie down on the floor while Dr. Nevin sewed up his bitten eyebrow.

Henry didn't share Betty's attachment to horses. (Theoretically, he said, he had a high opinion of them, but, in practice, he preferred a bicycle. Indeed, when they were young he had tried, unsuccessfully, to get Betty to share a tandem with him.) He was willing, though, to accompany her to Madison Square Garden horse shows when they could get away from the Vineyard, and he never complained about her annual Christmas gift to her favorite secretary, Florence "Bunny" Brown—a year's worth of hay for her horses.

Because they killed birds, cats were not as popular with either Henry or Betty, except when they were in trouble. In that case, a cat could always count on Hough help through an article describing its plight. So, although it was a cat story, Betty always liked recounting how Katharine Foote established the Animal Rescue League in Edgartown. Miss Foote had sailed directly into Edgartown (at that time, it was still served by a boat from the mainland). On her way down the gangplank she was met by a friend well acquainted with her devotion to animals, who called out that Katharine had arrived just in time to save a litter of kittens abandoned by the fisherman who had fed them until he left the island. Then and there, little Miss Foote, the first woman embalmer in Massachusetts (noted for having "laid out" the founder of Christian Science, Mary Baker Eddy) decided she would establish an animal shelter on the Vineyard. In winter, she arranged for visiting veterinarians. In summer, she coerced them to come to the island for the whole season. At first her combined shelter and hospital were in a house she rented on Edgartown's Main Street. In 1933, with her own $10,000, she built a shelter on the Edgartown–Vineyard Haven road. Among those who attended the opening was actress Katharine Cornell, a member of the shelter's board of directors. The shelter eventually was affiliated with the Massachusetts Society for the Prevention of Cruelty to Animals, which supplied a year-round vet.

When Katharine Foote died in 1955, the *Gazette* carried a front page, five-column obituary of the dauntless defender of animal rights. In later years, after it had came under MSPCA control, the shelter wasn't always what Henry would have liked it to be. In a letter to the MSPCA director in Boston, he wrote wistfully about how much he missed the compassion, the breadth of commitment, "the unstinted humanitarianism" of Katharine Foote's era.

Chapter 14

"Country Editor"

On the strength of the reviews garnered by *Martha's Vineyard: Summer Resort*, Hough acquired a literary agent. The agent urged him to write something autobiographical about life on the Vineyard, along the lines of Swedish writer Axel Munthe's best-selling *The Story of San Michele* about living with nature on Italy's Isle of Capri. But then the agent had another idea. The recent *Country Lawyer* by Bellamy Partridge was selling well. Henry had been thinking of writing a textbook on publishing a country newspaper; if "country" books were popular, this might be the time for a country-editor book, his agent suggested. Henry's proposal for one was accepted by Doubleday Doran. In the quiet, golden fall of 1939, while Betty went into the office, Henry spent mornings writing at home in his upstairs study. From then on, that was the pattern of their lives.

Enthusiastic about his project, Henry wrote 150 pages in ten days. He named his book *The Adventures of the Weekly Newspaper* and said, "It is supposed to represent a new viewpoint and to deny most of the accepted advice to country newspapermen, the great message being that you need not be bound by the rule, and the more clearly you run a country newspaper as you like, and as seems best for the community you are in, the better." The finished manuscript was in the hands of the publishers by New Year's Day, 1940, with publication scheduled for August. But that summer brought not just the usual mayhem on Martha's Vineyard. In Europe, Hitler's invasions had spread to the Netherlands, Belgium, and France; British forces had withdrawn from Dunkirk and Churchill had stirred his people and the world with his "blood, toil, tears and sweat" speech. It was hardly a promising time, Henry feared, for the success of a quiet book about living on an island and editing a country newspaper.

Country editor Henry Beetle Hough at work at a back-shop Linotype machine.
Copyright Alfred Eisenstaedt

Jack Scannell (foreground) and Walter Bettencourt of the *Gazette*'s "black gang" add a new roll of paper during a press run. *Photograph by Gretchen Van Tassel, courtesy of the* Vineyard Gazette

But the island newspaper editor-turned-author was mistaken. *New York Times* book reviewer J. Donald Adams called *Country Editor* "one of the most delectable books of the year." According to Lewis Gannett, in the *New York Herald Tribune,* as he read it he could "smell the sea breeze blowing across the harbor . . . and hear New England voices rich with Yankee humor." He listed it as one of the ten best books of the year, along with Walter van Tilburg Clark's *The Ox-Bow Incident,* Ernest Hemingway's *For Whom the Bell Tolls,* and Richard Wright's *Native Son.*

Henry was invited to New York for a radio interview on the popular "Information Please" program. The manager of Brentano's Bookstore in Philadelphia wrote to tell him the store's biggest window was featuring his book. (When *Country Editor* was reprinted in 1974, Chatham Press editor Chris Harris found when it was originally published Hough's book had scored above John F. Kennedy's *Why England Slept* and Hitler's *Mein Kampf* on several bestseller lists.)

Contrary to his fears, Hough's simple, quiet story of how two idealistic, indefatigable young newlyweds—with a minimum of money—made their country newspaper succeed was just what the public wanted. The book offered an escape from those terrifying, tumultuous times. In the early days of World War II, readers smiled over Betty's collie puppy Rikki chasing the bed of the *Gazette* press as it slid back and forth, and at stories of the Vineyard doctor who founded his own telephone company and shinnied up its poles in his tall silk hat to make line repairs. They accompanied Henry on his visits to the retired magazine editor who lived alone in her "Sylvan Hut" in the Indian Hill woods, with wild roses, blackberry vines, and sumac closing in around her kitchen door and a pot of black, thick soup that she called liquid bread always on the back of her Franklin stove.

The book's readers, facing an unknown future for a world at war, were reassured by Hough's description of days remembered not because anything special happened on them, but "because of the way the air felt, or because the trees across the street stood out with the sunlight on their branches and white clouds behind them."

As the reviews began to appear, Henry's Meat Packing Institute employer Pen Dudley wrote from New York: "How I would love to be there . . . to rejoice with you and Betty. You are to remember that Betty and I have probably believed in you more heartily than any other two living people. Just think how happy we are today."

Betty and George Sr. gave the book a coming-out party under the elm trees in Henry and Betty's Pierce Avenue yard. The invitations were sent out on a blank side of a sheet of the *Gazette*.

Country Editor was out of print within two years and was reprinted by the Council on Books in Wartime. In 1944 an Armed Forces edition printed 150,000 copies. Young men and women overseas read it and were reminded of their hometowns. At the Nuremberg Trials, German Foreign Minister Joachim von Ribbontrop, seeing a copy of it in the pocket of the American officer interrogating him, asked if he could read it when the officer was finished with it.

Some of those young soldiers who read the book abroad came home to be editors and editorial writers for such prestigious daily newspapers as the *New York Times* and the *Providence Journal*. They not only remembered reading *Country Editor* as a respite from battle, but also, in their later newspapering years, kept a copy of it as an inspiration in an office drawer. The *Vineyard Gazette*'s self-effacing co-editor thus influenced journalism nationwide.

With the success of *Country Editor*, Henry began to write fiction, inspired by his travels with his father to South Africa three years earlier.

Beginning in the 1920s, after their sons had finished college, George Hough Sr. and Abby Louise went on winter freighter cruises, not to Grand Tour countries like England, France, or Italy, but to the South Seas, Australia, and New Zealand. After Abby Louise's death in 1931, George Sr. had continued these cruises with George Jr.'s teenaged sons. In 1937, he invited his own younger son to be his travel companion, Henry's propensity for seasickness notwithstanding.

Henry was lukewarm about the idea, but Betty felt a trip would be a good escape for him from the increasingly heavy pressures of the paper, which seemed to be getting him down. He also was still disappointed by the failure to sell his typesetting machine. *Martha's Vineyard: Summer Resort* was doing well, but Betty felt Henry needed a distraction. In

Henry at his roll-top desk in the *Gazette*'s front office.
Photograph by Gretchen Van Tassel, courtesy of the Vineyard Gazette

December 1937, he and his father left from New Orleans on a cruise that continued until the end of March, taking them to all the major ports of South Africa.

George Hough Sr. and his younger son were, temperamentally, nearly exact opposites. Henry and his gentle, nature-loving mother had more in common. George Sr., particularly as the years progressed, was something of a bon vivant: he enjoyed fine food and drink, smoked the best of cigars, and didn't mind late nights. Henry, on the other hand, got seasick, never liked to travel, and thoroughly enjoyed small-town life. Even when he was not aboard a boat or ship, he had stomach troubles and they did not improve on the four-month cruise; indeed, he developed an ulcer. He was relieved whenever he found some place he could swim, or they put into a port with a milk bar, and when he could stay in a room where hot tea was served to guests in bed in the morning, as it often was in South African hotels. To make matters worse, just before Christmas, as he finished swimming one day, he injured his ankle and had to pack it in ice. For the rest of the cruise, he had to be careful with it.

Even so, Henry was open to all he saw and heard. Here he got an idea for a story about an adventurous black African boy from the Transkei "where the great rounded hills billow up toward the heavens and the white clouds billow down to the round hills until there seems little space between them," Henry wrote.

Soon after Henry returned home at last, his agent sold the story to *Esquire* magazine. An editor at Dial Press who read it proposed that Henry write an outline for a novel in the same setting. He was delighted with this suggestion, since fiction was what he longed to write. (One of his first published efforts had been a bleak short story about a castaway who eats his pet cat, printed in 1914 in the New Bedford High School magazine *Alpha*.) Henry started the South African novel soon after his return, but his first efforts were indifferently received and he abandoned the fiction project when he received the contract for *Country Editor*.

On the strength of that success, Hough returned to work on what became *That Lofty Sky*, the story of a Nazi cadet forced to leave his ship in South Africa, and his transformation into a new man by the goodness of a young Englishwoman.

Henry was brought up by a Victorian mother whom he worshiped; she would admonish her children, quoting Longfellow: "Life is real! Life is earnest! And the grave is not its goal." For the adult Henry, dealing with women as physical rather than spiritual beings— in life and in his fiction—was not easy. Asked when he was in his seventies for a comment on women, he looked befuddled. "Why," he replied, "women are the mothers of the race."

Women characters in his novels often seem uncomfortably added in, as if either Henry or an editor later decided they were needed. As far back as his Columbia days he had felt inhibited at showing admiration for a woman's physical attributes. In his 1963 novel *The Port,* his hero remarks, "I've always been afraid of the pretty ones, not afraid exactly, but uneasy. It is, of course, a primitive instinct for the male to seek the companionship of the lovely female under any and all circmstances, but it is also a primitive instinct, and one that sometimes prevails, for him to go by on the other side to avoid rather than to accept a challenge and the odds against him." Mary, in his 1947 *Long Anchorage*, is "as lovely as distant glory."

Henry tended to be courtly toward women all his life and self-conscious about their sexuality. Betty was strong, determined, and intelligent, but self-conscious, too, about things physical. Henry needed Betty's determination and firmness to succeed as a writer; he and the paper both benefited from her political liberalism. She needed his quiet, understated humor to enliven her seriousness and keep her explosive, tart temper in check, as well as his social skills to make life beyond the workplace bearable. Theirs was a devoted but complex relationship. Intimacy in the bedroom, as much as can be determined, was not an important part of it. They might argue and shout at each other in the *Gazette* office but, minutes later, walking on Main Street, a gentle, fragile Betty would be clinging to her Henry's arm. Keen editor that she was, Betty recognized and nurtured her husband's writing abilities, and protected and defended him from all criticism but her own. If a reviewer disliked what he had written, she would go after him with all the ferocity of a guard dog.

Some speculated that George Sr. recognized the fire burning within his star *New Bedford Evening Standard* reporter and, understanding that his brilliant but unsure-of-himself son needed such a life partner, had persuaded a hesitant Betty to take Henry's courtship seriously.

However unconventional their marriage, unquestionably the brightest moments of Henry's cruise were Betty's loving cablegrams with news of Captain Matrix and of doings back home in Edgartown:

"Let me know how you are. All well. Business OK. We need to hasten your return. . . . Be sure you have a good time. Do not let matters worry you."

"Mats is a very little baby compared to Al's roughneck who hazes him rather hard at times. Matsy comes to me for help, but is just as rough himself when he gets a chance."

"Mats upset the box with all the little squares of cardboard used in makeup. Goodnight, darling. Only a little more than two months more, I hope."

"Mr. Pent went away Thursday and has not come back and Mrs. Pent has phoned his usual haunts without result. She is nervous."

"The weather is really cold this evening, in the 20s, but beautiful and still. A small moon."

"Matsy and I had a walk in Sheriff's Meadow. Good night, darling. I have had a light put right over your typewriter."

But it was a weary, not a rested Henry, who came back to Edgartown. His incipient stomach problem had turned into an ulcer that plagued him on and off for many years.

Henry and Betty
at a *Gazette*
office window.
*Copyright Alfred
Eisenstaedt*

In 1939, when German armies marched into Poland and World War II began, Betty asked Henry, as the *Gazette* was about to go to press, if the paper shouldn't take notice of the war in some way, despite its island-only policy. They agreed that it should, because the war's outbreak was weighing as heavily on island minds as anywhere else in the world. Henry set a few paragraphs about how Vineyard residents had heard over their radios that morning of the bombing of Warsaw and the invasion of Poland. And then he described how the last hovering clouds of a northeast storm had drawn away and unveiled a crystal, gilded morning: "I put in what kind of day it was in order that future generations might know, if they cared to look back in the files, what things were like on our Island on that day when the world went mad," Henry wrote.

Throughout the war, the Houghs threw themselves and the paper into the war effort with patriotic zeal. Betty had already established a reputation for fundraising: in 1938, she set up a *Gazette* relief fund to help with the devastation all across the island when a hurricane washed away much of the Vineyard's Menemsha fishing community, killed one person, injured several, and damaged property to the amount of about half a million dollars. Her Gazette Hurricane Relief Fund successfully raised more than $12,000 to help those in need, through story after story of flooded homes, damaged crops, and battered boats, and turrets and porches blown from houses. (Characteristically, she paid no attention to objections from the Red Cross to her independent fundraising.)

Betty mounted similar campaigns for contributions to the Red Cross War Fund and for the War Dog Fund, which provided sentry dogs for the armed forces. Betty used Matrix as the vehicle for soliciting for the Dog Fund, and the campaign on the island was so successful that in recognition of Matsy's services, he was promoted by national fund officials from private to sergeant to lieutenant, and finally to captain. Matsy was also a symbolic fundraiser for the National Canine Defence League of London, England, which needed money for English dogs affected by the conflict. To raise funds, the league sold valuable United States stamps to English collectors. Matsy's role was to get the *Gazette*'s far-flung subscribers to donate these stamps with his "tail wags of enthusiasm and gratitude" and through headlines like "Buy Bones for an English Towser, Says Captain Matrix." Though some readers found all this puerile, and even Betty herself once said to a young mother, "You're lucky to have children so you don't make a fool of yourself over a dog," most simply smiled at the *Gazette* co-editor's imagination and gave to this Matrix cause or that. Even the Vineyard's American Legion Post made Captain Matrix its official mascot for his "commendable service to our country."

Betty's relentless money-seeking for these campaigns was in addition to superintending regular *Gazette* news coverage and editing all the copy. It was little wonder that she dealt snappily with advertisers and subscribers who were tardy with bill payments—and with anyone else who, wittingly or unwittingly, annoyed her. To the head of the electric company who was slow in paying for his ad, she acidly wrote, "We paid cash for our refrigerator. Now send us a check for your ad." Although she knew better, Betty sometimes could not control her outspokenness. So even though the Houghs were devoted to the national cause, when the Office of War Information deluged the *Gazette* with releases they couldn't use, in 1943 Betty replied: "We hear from the government every day asking us to save newsprint in every possible way. This is hardly necessary since advertising has virtually disappeared and we are down to a poor eight-page paper anyhow. But then comes the stream of mats and copy. Well, we must take care of the Selective Service stories, the Red Cross surgical dressings, the

Red Cross War Fund, the rationing, the blackout and dim-out rules and modifications, recurring angles of the salvage and conservation progress, the USO and a lot of other matters which are tied in closely to our own people. We have to keep War Bonds and Stamps before them as much as possible. And all this doesn't allow for any of the run-of-the-mill information or propaganda which comes into this office. We throw up our hands and drop the bulk of it into the wastebasket."

Items about islanders serving their country overseas did not go into the wastebasket, however; Betty established a page devoted to news from and about them, and called it Along Far Flung Fronts. Blood Drive announcements were not thrown out either. All *Gazette* staff members did what they could for the war effort, along with the rest of the island. Joe Allen signed up for the State Guard and Bill Roberts for the ration board, Betty took a Red Cross course, and Henry planted a victory garden. Both Betty and Henry became airplane spotters.

Even tree-loving Betty did not complain when a stand of scrub oaks was cut down by the Navy on the Great Plain to make a flying field for training carrier pilots. She and Henry were less understanding, however, of all the low-flying planes the war brought to the island. They even suggested, tongue in cheek, when the weathervane on top of the Edgartown Congregational Church steeple was found bent one morning, that the damage might have been caused by a low-flying aircraft. They were also on the side of the Katama dairy farmer whose fences were bulldozed down by the Navy to make way for an aerial gunner range. His cows invaded neighborhood gardens and caused considerable damage.

In the summer of 1942, seventy-foot patrol torpedo (PT) boats appeared in island waters and their crews were warmly welcomed. At the Edgartown Yacht Club, a gala party honored the young sailors. In turn, wishing to show appreciation for Edgartown hospitality, they foolishly dropped two depth charges as a farewell salute. The first one exploded in deep water outside the harbor, and all was well; the second was let go within the harbor and did not fall deep enough to explode. And there, dangerously, it lay. Strict self-censorship rules meant the *Gazette* could not report on the movement of Navy vessels. But a depth charge near small boats was, obviously, something fishermen and yachtsmen should know about. The Houghs weighed their duty to the government against their duty to the local population, and the local population won out.

The censorship code, as they read it, prohibited reporting the movement of naval vessels. "But we did not regard PT boats as vessels any more than we did catboats or cabin cruisers," Henry wrote, so the paper reported the location of the unexploded depth charge dropped by the PT boat. Immediately, Boston papers were after the story, and Navy officials accused the Houghs of endangering their activities.

In the end, wisdom prevailed. Edgartown's selectmen appealed to the Navy for the bomb's removal. A Hough editorial pointed out that dropping the depth charge was an

Henry with Broadway actress Katharine Cornell.
Photograph by Howard Wall, courtesy of the Vineyard Gazette

outrage to public safety. A week or so later, the Navy sent a removal squad back to Edgartown and hired a local fisherman to drag for the charge. In the mucky bottom, however, it could not be retrieved; a second charge was dropped to blow up the first one. When the danger was past, the head of the Office of Censorship sent the Houghs a letter rebuking them for publicizing secret naval movements.

The camaraderie of the war years also brought the Houghs into contact with notable visitors they might not have known otherwise. In 1942 the English writer W. Somerset Maugham, taking refuge from England, summered on the Vineyard; during his visit the film based on his *The Moon and Sixpence* had its world premiere. Henry and Betty were invited to cocktails and dinner with him before the Edgartown screening. Henry made brief introductory remarks at it and later interviewed him for the *Gazette.*

"Mr. Maugham likes the bathing here," Henry reported, "but he says quite candidly that it does not come up to that of the Riviera. . . . So far as he has observed, the Vineyard water is not so blue. Comparison with the English Channel, though, is all in the Vineyard's favor."

The Houghs took Maugham to Fish Hook for a visit with Henry's father. During his island stay, Maugham was editing the book *Introduction to Modern English and American Literature*. In the introduction to the poetry section Maugham remembered how, "The day before I wrote these lines I was wandering along a dirt road on Martha's Vineyard," and compared the delight of seeing a flowering Vineyard tree to the effect of reading poetry.

That summer Katharine Cornell performed on the stage of the Tisbury gym for the benefit of the USO. Though the Houghs had met her before through their mutual interest in animals (Miss Cornell had dachshunds), they became close friends in the intimacy of the war years.

Chapter 16

Of Hurricanes and Steamships and Peace

In the midst of the war in September 1944 another hurricane struck the Vineyard. Despite the reports coming through that Thursday the 14th, no one wanted to believe that the lovely, sunny autumn afternoon would have an angry end. Just in case, however, the *Gazette* staff worked late, setting type and partly making up the forms for printing. If the storm was as fierce as the hurricane of '38—when Joe Allen had to write his copy in the garage by the beams from his car headlights—electric power was likely to be lost. Then printing the paper would be impossible. The *Gazette* had never missed an issue since its founding in 1846; Henry, Betty, and Bill Roberts wanted to keep that record. They considered returning to work after Thursday evening supper and printing the paper then, but decided against it. The wind blowing as Henry walked Matsy home was a southeast one; rain usually accompanies sou'easters on the Vineyard, but such storms pass in twelve hours or so. On her way home from a meeting with fellow Edgartown Library trustees, Betty saw unsettling lightning flashes and felt the wind picking up, even stronger than in the '38 hurricane. By then it was too late to print the paper. The Houghs spent a mostly sleepless night watching the streetlights go out along Pierce Avenue and the "wild dance"of the mulberry tree at their gate.

On Friday morning disaster was everywhere. The mulberry tree still stood, but branches of their stately elms littered the garden. Henry and Betty walked down Main Street to the waterfront. There, the big black Manxman, the largest yawl in the world, had been flung across the harbor and taken a fishing schooner with it. In the streets, fallen trees and limbs blocked traffic. Here and there, wind-driven trees had crashed through rooftops and whacked off chimneys. At the *Gazette*, the Houghs found that indomitable Joe Allen already had made his way from Vineyard Haven to leave his account of the storm's effects there.

Joseph Chase Allen, the *Gazette*'s "Wheelhouse Loafer," in his home office on Vineyard Haven's Main Street. *Courtesy of the* Vineyard Gazette

But without electricity his story could not be typeset or the paper printed.

The Houghs, Bill Roberts, and Everett Gale, the pressman, discussed putting together a mimeographed sheet, but discarded the idea. But Betty announced they had no choice in the matter—they had to find some way to print the paper. Bill and Henry began phoning mainland newspapers to see if they could use someone else's printing facilities. But most of these—including George Hough Jr.'s *Falmouth Enterprise*—had lost their electricity, too. Finally, a former New Bedford newspaperman turned printer was found. In his small shop—big enough for typesetting but not for printing the *Gazette*—Henry and Bill were told they could finish setting their copy. The paper would be late, but it might come out after all.

Hough and Bill Roberts took an early boat to New Bedford and finished their typesetting. That evening, Betty sent Everett Gale to the mainland with his car filled with the printing forms "locked up" on Thursday, along with new copy on the hurricane she and Joe had written. Bill and Henry set it, but they still hadn't located a printing press with power. Finally, on Sunday, they found a press in Plymouth with power and a welcome for the Vineyarders. By Monday morning, after a long weekend, Friday's *Gazette* was, at last, on the boat going back to the island.

Meanwhile, Allied parachutists were landing in Holland; Henry sheepishly admitted later that he was so preoccupied with the Vineyard's hurricane damage and the *Gazette's* production problem that he was largely oblivious of the news beyond. But less than a year later came the event no one could ignore.

Gazette lore maintained that, somehow, the most important events occurred at just the right time to make the paper. August 14, 1945, was a Tuesday. At 8 a.m. that day, as Henry set the final type for the Tuesday *Gazette* (a smaller summer edition, added in 1929 to the regular full-scale Friday paper), he reported how the end of World War II was heralded on the Vineyard.

As he did at the outbreak of the war, and at the D-Day invasion (when at Betty's instigation he called Edgartown ministers to request the ringing of church bells), Henry chose to describe the island at the moment the world news came. Out in the back shop on V-J Day, the Linotype clicked and shuffled as Hough wrote of the light fog that was covering almost everything in Edgartown that morning. But there were a few bright spots overhead, he wrote, that suggested that soon the sun would break through. "All the daily occupations are begun. The Island is awake and busy and the summer people are getting up. The radios are turned on for broadcasts of late news. . . . So the faraway victory comes which is the most immediate thing to every living soul, and makes the commonplace on this morning full of excitement and pleasure."

Spontaneous parades formed that night in Vineyard Haven, Oak Bluffs, and Edgartown. Fire sirens and horns sounded and homemade confetti showered on paraders.

In Vineyard Haven, shotguns were fired and conch shells "dragged from some forgotten corner" were blown. In Edgartown, schoolchildren led the parade and Circuit Avenue, the main street in Oak Bluffs, overflowed with people. The following Sunday, island churches were full. All beaches were open again (some had been closed for landing craft practice). At last, Henry wrote, "cares and apprehensions were forgotten."

During the war, both the three-decker steamship *Naushon*, the grandest of the boats serving the Vineyard and Nantucket, and the vessel *New Bedford* had crossed the Atlantic to serve their country. The *Naushon* became a hospital ship in the British Navy and the *New Bedford* had helped in a rescue when other boats in its convoy were torpedoed. Islanders expected both vessels soon to be steaming again along their regular routes. Instead, the boatline owner and operator, the New Haven Railroad, announced that it was selling to new owners. The *Naushon* and *New Bedford* would be replaced by a Hudson River ferry ill-equipped to make crossings in the open waters of Vineyard and Nantucket sounds.

Islanders were dumbfounded, the more so to learn that the buyer, Massachusetts Steamship Lines, had eliminated direct connections with the trains to the Woods Hole and New Bedford docks from out of state. Passengers taking the train from New York or Providence could no longer buy through tickets to the Vineyard. No freight originating outside Massachusetts could go aboard steamship-line vessels unless a Massachusetts transfer agent was involved—which meant delays in receiving freight and spending more money for it.

Something had to be done, so the Houghs became champions in the battle against the new line. "We've got to fight now as we never fought before, every Vineyarder, every Nantucketer, and every lover of the Islands," Hough wrote. "Without prior consultation, without proper knowledge of the needs of the Islands and their recreational industry and fisheries, without real experience in this unique situation, the Massachusetts Steamship Lines have chosen to limit their transportation service to intrastate operation."

Three years later, the contretemps ended with the creation of a state-run boatline with a five-member board, two of them with Vineyard connections, including Stephen Carey Luce of Vineyard Haven, the patriarchal president of Martha's Vineyard National Bank and the hospital, and an advisor to the railroad when it had operated the boatline.

For the moment, the fight for a better boatline had been won. "But no one need ever try to tell us," Hough wrote when victory was assured, "that a newspaper crusade is easy, or good fun, or exhilarating." And soon the victory proved a hollow one. Island relations quickly soured with the new line (the New Bedford, Woods Hole, Martha's Vineyard and Nantucket Steamship Authority).

By 1951, the city of New Bedford was in decline. The textile industry, the city's mainstay after its whaling era, had moved to the South. The New Bedford stores islanders once frequented for up-to-date shopping were closing. Fewer Vineyarders now needed the boat

Menemsha, the day after the 1944 hurricane. *Courtesy of the* Vineyard Gazette

to New Bedford for their off-island errands, preferring to shop and drive in Cape Cod's Falmouth and Hyannis, now busy towns. The boatline, suffering a deficit, raised taxes in the communities it served, with islanders forced to pay a disproportionate share.

The Houghs and Stephen Carey Luce waged a new battle to free the Vineyard of the coffer-draining link to New Bedford. The fight took on a very personal tone. The *New Bedford Standard,* Henry's father's newspaper, had been replaced by the *New Bedford Evening Standard Times,* with a publisher imported from the Midwest. The new paper, in Hough estimation, was a far cry in editorial integrity from the old. Furthermore, the *Standard Times,* eager to lend economic support to its home city, zealously supported keeping New Bedford on the steamship line. Henry's editorials almost as often attacked the *Standard Times* and its publisher as they did the boat company. Finally, eight years later, New Bedford service was discontinued.

But even that was not the end of the story. In 1978, beside himself at how mass tourism, promoted by the Authority (and even, some said, by Henry's writings, too), was harming the island way of life, Hough criticized the agency he had helped create. The Authority, he felt, had abandoned its original premise: an agency controlled by the Vineyard and Nantucket and serving their economic, social, and cultural needs. "Compared to what it was intended to be," he wrote, "it has turned into a caricature of a monster."

Chapter 17

Journalists of Tomorrow

Although Henry and Betty Hough had no children, young people became part of their *Gazette* lives. The first of them was Caroline Rabell, a teenager from New York City whose family summered in Oak Bluffs. She simply walked into the *Gazette* office one day (a decade or so after the Houghs had become editors) and applied for a job "with such direct logic and interest that we could think of no reason for turning her down," Hough said. She was ready and willing to solicit advertising, read proof, or wrap papers, though reporting, of course, appealed the most. She spent two summers on the paper, as did generations of young reporters after her.

After Caroline, the three Woollcott sisters from Baltimore—Joan, Barbara, and Polly—came to the *Gazette* one after the other as cub reporters. They were nieces of the *New Yorker* columnist and drama critic Alexander Woollcott, the model for the protagonist of Kaufman and Hart's Broadway hit *The Man Who Came to Dinner*. The girls' grandparents summered in Vineyard Haven.

The Woollcott sisters—and the other cubs who came after them—covered Edgartown Yacht Club races, Oak Bluffs band concerts and community sings, and the West Tisbury Agricultural Fair. They examined hotel registers to see what illustrious visitors were visiting the island, and perhaps interviewed them. They might be assigned an ambassador, a leading song writer, an eminent scientist, an author, an actor. Polly Woollcott interviewed author Thornton Wilder, vacationing in Chilmark. Howard W. Young, still a student at Choate when he became a *Gazette* summer reporter, spent an afternoon talking with James Cagney.

Betty, pink-cheeked, blue-eyed, and prematurely white-haired, usually in blue sneakers, a denim skirt, an open-necked blouse, and a cardigan, ruled over the *Gazette*'s sunny "city room." There she patiently, meticulously, demandingly reviewed her staff's copy at her work table, where her typewriter was nearly submerged under papers, clippings, letters, and books. Since she used the floor as her filing cabinet, papers and letters were strewn there, too. A dog's water bowl was never far away, though its canine owner was more likely to be slumbering in his master's quieter, less cluttered office. Clutter around Betty was of no concern; she thrived on it, and always knew exactly where anything was. Clutter in a reporter's copy, however, was mercilessly excised with a soft black pencil. Every one of her trainees—many of whom went on to careers with major newspapers and magazines, including the *New York Herald Tribune*, the *New York Times*, the *Providence Journal*, the *Ladies' Home Journal*, *This Week* and *Life* magazines, and the *New Yorker*—recognized her as a brilliant city editor with a nose for the facts and a strong sense of story structure. She quickly learned

Betty Hough, matriarch of the *Gazette* newsroom, among her papers, clippings, and books. *Courtesy of the* Vineyard Gazette

Henry's father, George A. Hough ("Pat" in his later years), with *Gazette* intern Polly Woollcott. *Courtesy of Chris Murphy*

her staff's strengths and weaknesses, and sought out her interns' interests, assigning them related stories. She patiently waited for interns to develop into reporters. If they couldn't type, she accepted their handwritten copy for a week or two until they learned. (She had only the rudiments of typing herself; like Henry, she never learned to type with more than two fingers.) Friday afternoon, once the paper had come out, she would dispatch one of her young "keeds," as she called them, to the Corner Drugstore to buy ice cream cones or popsicles for all. At the end of the work day, she drove home to Pierce Avenue while Henry walked home with the dog.

There Betty would fret about the company her young staff was keeping after *Gazette* hours. In her estimation, no one was good enough for her charges. Ultimately, however, sometimes long after their *Gazette* years, when her interns finally married, she tried to be accepting and, once children arrived, welcoming of the new generation. When former reporter Peter Bunzel and his wife Jane asked them to be godparents of two of their sons, the Houghs were concerned they might not be good role models, since they both had become agnostics. Betty, with the stronger religious upbringing of the couple—her father had been a pillar of Uniontown's St. Peter's Episcopal Church—took matters like godparenting seriously. Though both Houghs were awkward with young children, in later years Henry enjoyed entertaining them with such corny, old-fashioned jokes as "Mrs. Bigger had a baby. Who was bigger, Mrs. Bigger or her baby?" Few questioned why the Houghs themselves had elected not to have a family. Most thought their decision had been right: Betty might cluck maternally and nurture her young office charges, but her first allegiance, always, was to the *Gazette.*

The *Gazette* staff of the 1940s, including Captain Matrix.
Back row, from left: Everett Gale, Henry Hough, Bill Roberts, Lenny Belisle, Joe Allen.
Front row, from left: Marion Roberts, Jean Morgan, Betty Hough, Florence Brown,
Walter Bettencourt. *Courtesy of the* Vineyard Gazette

Only occasionally did Henry participate in cub reporter training. Once he achieved
some success with his writing, he would stay at home mornings to work on his current book
or story instead of coming into the office. Without the income from his writing, they never
could have managed financially, Betty frequently said. So it was usually 11 a.m. or after
lunch when Henry seated himself in his dark front office at the roll-top desk, decorated
with a picture of Betty and a print of Joseph Pulitzer. He wrote his editorials then, hos-
pitably received prestigious visitors, proudly showed off the *Gazette's* back shop, and sometimes dealt with the irate public who probably would have become more irate if Betty had
talked to them in her candid way.

For all her peaches-and-cream grandmotherly looks, Betty brooked no nonsense, no
matter how important an official might be or how valuable an advertiser. Anyone who

crossed Betty Hough or was insufficiently appreciative of Henry had no future with the *Gazette*. Henry, with his many community connections—he was historian and president of the Dukes County Historical Society, on the Edgartown School Committee, and a board member of the Martha's Vineyard National Bank, Martha's Vineyard Hospital, and the Edgartown Board of Trade—often had to soothe hurt feelings when Betty offended someone. He tended to do this by nodding agreeably and saying "Of course," with his New England accent affecting the "r" in "course."

"Betty almost courted unpopularity," Peter Bunzel, the former reporter, recalled. "She was rebellious about the people on the Vineyard whom she didn't think liked the paper enough. There was a kind of arrogance in her attitude. Anyone who wasn't a keeper of the Vineyard she was against, and that included many of the merchants who wanted to expand the Vineyard beyond its environmental limits." She was rarely short-tempered with *Gazette* interns, but often with Henry. In exasperation, he would sometimes stamp into his office, his brown eyes flashing, and slam the door. As one who often suffered from Betty's sharp tongue, he would try, in a hesitant, self-conscious way, to mollify a reporter he thought Betty's sharp (though probably correct) criticism had wounded. (Although Henry also could be fierce-tempered, he usually saved his ire for matters he considered important.) Mostly he sought to teach the young reporters simply by the example he set.

Both Houghs were strict grammarians and insisted on a thoughtful use of the English language. In his *Gazette* style sheet, Hough wrote: "There must be vigilance against the trite and repetitious. . . . Vogue words must be avoided. 'Trigger' and 'spark' used as verbs are to be shunned. . . . The lingo of social scientists and other specialists demands translation. . . . Never write groom for bridegroom; a groom is a horse's attendant." No "widows" appeared in the *Gazette*, only "wives of the late. . . ." Furthermore, women were women and not "ladies." Betty also decreed—since Henry had become prematurely bald while she became prematurely white—that no word portrait of an interview subject include the word "bald," even if the subject was bald.

"Once," Bunzel remembered, "Henry called me into his office and gave me a grammar lesson. He handled it with such diplomacy. 'This is a paper that cares about literacy and writing,' he said, 'and I want you to be careful.' And Betty wasn't to know about it, Henry emphasized. It all took place behind closed doors. Chastisement with great feeling."

When an Edgartown socialite bustled in to talk about the flowers blooming in her garden, Henry patiently heard her out. The column about the garden he then produced made the flowers virtually glow, and taught a young reporter the importance of listening.

But along with teaching their fledglings to write, the Houghs were instilling their ideals of integrity in journalism and their respect for the natural world. Sometimes on Sundays, Henry would take them walking in the Fish Hook woods and for visits with his crusty but inspiring father. Impressionable cub reporters usually finished their stint at the *Gazette*

A cheerful crew at work in the *Gazette*'s back shop; Betty Hough is in the center. *Courtesy of the* Vineyard Gazette

believing in most of the causes the Houghs believed in and fought for. "Mrs. Hough was the mother of my mind," one intern reported.

She encouraged her reporters to take stands on the issues of the day, from local to world concerns, and she was not above goading them into commitment when they seemed to waver. Even though the *Gazette* concentrated on island matters, the Houghs kept informed about state, national, and international issues and expected their reporters to do the same.

"In the morning, after Mrs. Hough had spent an evening absorbing new information, the atmosphere in the *Gazette* office crackled with her comments and she expected answers, which is not to say she expected debaters' rebuttals. In all her conversations, she liked the flow of talk to move forward . . . in a gradual enrichment of the subject," assistant editor Colbert Smith remembered, in a tribute to Betty after her death.

Writing to the *Wells College Chronicle* in 1940, Betty described her activities with her "youngsters."

"I direct their activities in the summer, which means acting as dictionary and encyclopedia for them as well as telling them where people live and why they are famous and picking out countless stories for them at which to try their skill. . . . But they are all alive and keen and stars of a kind. . . .

"In addition, I proof read, much against my will, do a lot of address changing, campaigns by mail for circulation, review books and do a little bookkeeping. . . . I read and edit all copy and get fussier and fussier as the years roll on. But no use trying to be a perfectionist, and it can't be done anyhow if one is to have diversity and individuality in the work."

She directed her young reporters to look for human interest stories where "little things happen. A great deal of interesting news is in small ocean races," she pointed out. Reporters should encourage people to tell them things, she also advised. "A lot that anyone tells a reporter is valueless and must be disregarded," she said, "but out of the whole comes a valuable harvest. The big chance will never come unless you are alert to all the small chances."

Henry and Betty, though registered Republicans, were Independents, and liberal politically; "pink," a number of people in town called them. Because of its selective membership policies, the Houghs scorned the Edgartown Yacht Club socially, though they reported all of its races and events. They were proud to number among their friends American Civil Liberties Union founder and president Roger Baldwin, who had a Chilmark house; and Roosevelt-appointed Tennessee Valley Authority director David Lilienthal. Warmly welcomed as a neighbor, Lilienthal bought a parcel of North Tisbury land from George Hough Sr.

In addition to championing animals and nature through Henry's editorials and Betty's "bushels" of copy, the Houghs supported those in need. Every Christmas Betty urged readers to give to the Red Stocking Fund, which put gifts under the trees of needy Vineyard children. In summer, she sought vacation homes for the poor children of New York City by writing moving stories about the *Herald Tribune* Fresh Air Fund. When the Martha's Vineyard Hospital tried to transfer monies to general hospital funds from a gift that provided, in perpetuity, a free bed for the locally needy, she intervened.

As the *Gazette* grew in renown and Henry was increasingly recognized as a writer, the Houghs were courted by the many notable people who visited the island. Though they enjoyed the attention, they never forgot that their first obligation was to their year-round neighbors. However, the Houghs usually concentrated on the people and affairs of Edgartown, leaving Oak Bluffs, West Tisbury, and Vineyard Haven to Joe Allen; the island's "rural" dwellers, in Chilmark and Gay Head, sometimes wondered if the *Gazette* cared about them at all.

One of Betty's greatest sources of Edgartown information was Florence Scott Brown, hired as secretary and general factotum when she was a young divorced mother. Like Joe Allen, Bill Roberts, and Everett Gale, Bunny Brown would spend her life at the *Gazette*. Her ear became fine-tuned to news as well as gossip. Her infinite knowledge of local names and relationships provided just the right link with the working Edgartown population.

Just as she handled and instructed her cub reporters, Betty dealt with the club secretaries and town columnists, though perhaps with a little more impatience than with her young people. They had been an integral part of the *Gazette* even before the Houghs' purchase; under Betty's tutelage, amateurs though they were, their writing skills were honed. As a result, their columns were rarely mundane and often charming. Mrs. Napoleon Madison of the island's Gay Head Wampanoags, for example, recounted the doings of her community with intimacy and narrative skill: "Gay Head: There she lies before us, a huge promontory rising up from the blue waters of Menemsha Bight and Menemsha Pond, with never a change except as the 'swift seasons roll.' With never a change, did someone say? Well, never a change save the houses, which seem to be increasing year by year."

Sometimes the columnists would mail their work, written longhand, into the *Gazette* office. At other times, pleased to be associated with the Vineyard newspaper, they would hand-deliver their copy and stop for a not-so-welcome chat—particularly trying on the busy day before publication.

But an eve-of-publication arrival who was always welcomed was tireless Joe Allen, an imposing presence—tall, sturdy, and usually carrying a cowboy hat. He would lean against the big black safe acquired from the Oak Bluffs post office, the centerpiece of Betty Hough's city room, and inform her in a booming voice of the island doings she would soon be reading about in his copy. He would banter, tell tall stories, and tease, to Betty's amusement—though she would never admit it. In 1956, when she had broken an arm and was out of the office for a time, he wrote for her:

Florence "Bunny" Scott Brown, *Gazette* secretary and general factotum,
had an unfailingly good ear for Edgartown news and gossip.
Courtesy of the Vineyard Gazette

Glooms of dark, deep purple overspread the office now.
There's not a thing that seems exactly right.
For never voice is lifted in profane and heated row,
Nor rolls a fresh-dug eyeball from a fight.
Uncanny is this atmosphere so peaceful that it pains;
Oh, give us back our battlefield with blood and smoke and stains,
'Tis hard to wait till Mrs. H. returns.

Chapter 18

A Splendid Symbiotic Relationship

As much as the Houghs valued the *Gazette*'s young reporters, their training was a sideline for Henry and Betty. They believed their primary role as journalists was to preserve the Vineyard, and grappled with one conservation crisis after another.

After the war, driving increasingly became a way of life in the nation, especially with President Dwight D. Eisenhower's highway expansion and improvement. More drivers on better roads brought more visitors, with their cars, to the Vineyard; island businesses wanted to accommodate them, with more and bigger roads, signs, and lodgings.

Even before the war the *Gazette* had confronted the issue of signs and billboards on the island. The Pacific Oil Company of Fall River opened a filling station on the harbor front in Vineyard Haven and erected billboards to advertise it. However, in defense of the Vineyard tradition of no billboards, the Garden Club and the *Gazette*'s Joe Allen immediately protested. An oil company spokesman apologized, explaining that the company was not aware of Vineyard sentiment about billboards, and pledged to reduce the size of the signs.

In the fifties, large directional signs to historic sites were erected by the state to guide island newcomers. Objecting, again, to the size of the signs, the *Gazette* urged Joseph A. Sylvia, state representative, to intercede on behalf of the Vineyard; these signs too were scaled down as a result of *Gazette* intervention.

Next, operators of big tour buses complained that the natural arches of trees above the roads were dangerous; the drivers had to swerve to avoid them. Betty countered that, economically and aesthetically, tour buses were destructive. Henry, quoting the long-established policy of the Martha's Vineyard Garden Club in an editorial, pointed out that "the Vineyard has always had and should always have trees beside the road, the closer the better, with due regard for safety and the actual needs of road construction. We should certainly not be bound here by rules and precepts worked out for through routes of the mainland, for over-size buses, and for high-speed traffic. Arches of trees and arches of summer shade are especially to be desired. One great aim is the effect of country, to be found less and less in the modern world—country and countryside, not held at arm's length, but reaching out to the beholder.

"The limitations which size has placed on the Island should be turned to advantage in all respects such as these; we are not a through route from anywhere to anywhere else; the greatest asset we have for sale is an attractiveness different in quality and kind from that of the mainland and often requiring special measures to conserve it; all our ways are scenic drives and none predominately commercial. The hedgerows and natural arches of trees should be symbols of what can be and should be accomplished."

When Vineyard beach erosion from winter storms became a concern, the *Gazette* was in the forefront of efforts to control it. *Photograph by Alison Shaw, courtesy of the* Vineyard Gazette

Stone walls on Martha's Vineyard narrowly escaped being ground up for road reinforcement by an off-island rock-crushing firm. *Courtesy of the* Vineyard Gazette

In the 1960s, these up-island hedges came under attack; early one fall, state Department of Public Works employees began cutting them. Betty, Henry, and the Garden Club objected. The *Gazette* recounted the history of the hedgerows, reminding readers how just after the war Joseph Sylvia, the state representative, had obtained $50,000 to maintain their proper trimming—partly because "so many distinguished visitors to the Island, including senators and governors . . . have, without exception, expressed admiration for the hedgerows." Henry also noted that articles about the island's unique style of hedge trimming had appeared in magazines and mainland newspapers. The paper begged Vineyarders to help save the hedges. In the uproar that followed, the DPW admitted its mistake and stopped cutting, explaining that the intention was only to remove the hedgerows where they obstructed speed and traffic signs.

In the 1950s, when winter storms and gales swept away dunes and beaches, erosion became a major island concern. The Chilmark Town Affairs Committee invited the dean of the College of Engineering at New York University to look over areas of extensive erosion and suggest a remedy. When he proposed a survey of island erosion, with the cost shared by federal, state, and county governments, Henry warmly endorsed the idea.

"This is not something that can be deferred indefinitely," Henry wrote, noting that the state should shoulder some of the responsibility because of the importance of the island to the general economy of the Commonwealth and because of the value of island shellfisheries, which erosion was harming. Ultimately, state and federal engineers did make a preliminary study.

Beach acquisition, as well as preservation, was a *Gazette* concern of the 1940s and 1950s. In 1941 Joseph Sylvia proposed state purchase of the sweeping crescent of beach between Oak Bluffs and Edgartown. This land was owned by the Hart family of New Britain, Connecticut, as well as the adjoining family settlement called Harthaven, along with other New Britain manufacturing families. For years, they allowed the public free access but, as island land values increased, the family asked the state or county to buy it, if public use continued. Sylvia and Betty persuaded the state to make the purchase, with county management to prevent possible future exploitation of the land.

The acquisition was not completed until fifteen years later. In the middle of the process, the state ran out of money for such acquisitions and, under blind names, an Edgartown developer began buying what the state had not yet purchased, planning a major waterfront development. Betty was alerted and, again with Sylvia's aid, informed the state Department of Natural Resources of the beach's importance to the community. The developer's land was taken by eminent domain. Henry hailed the acquisition as a milestone of island history. Similarly, a decade later, *Gazette* publicity helped win for the public a small stretch of beach on Vineyard Haven harbor where construction of a twenty-apartment building had been proposed.

When the owners of the *New Bedford Standard Times*—the newcomers since Henry's father's day—wanted to erect a television tower at the Gay Head Cliffs, the *Gazette* compared their planned "colossus" to the Eiffel Tower, the Washington Monument, and the Empire State Building, then the tallest building in the world; the structure planned for little Gay Head, the *Gazette* noted, was only 226 feet lower. The tower was not built.

In the last quarter of the nineteenth century, a tidy little red Seamen's Bethel was built on the approach to the boat dock in Vineyard Haven. In the days when schooners from Down East put into the harbor regularly, it welcomed visiting seamen. The bethel chaplain brought the sailors ashore on his small boat, and offered them hospitality after a long voyage. The mission provided a chapel, easy chairs and books, and eventually a telephone. In 1957, an off-island realty trust company planned to buy the bethel and convert it into a

The entire *Gazette* staff spent Friday mornings in the back shop assembling and mailing out newspapers. Betty and Henry Hough are in the foreground; Dixie Hill, center. *Courtesy of the* Vineyard Gazette

refreshment and souvenir stand. Most of the activities of the mission would move a half mile away to the former Marine Hospital. But the strength of public outcry, Garden Club suggestions of how the bethel could stay in place, and *Gazette* editorials kept the historic structure in its waterfront location for three decades more. (During this time, the chapel remained open to the public; when the building was finally moved and attached to the American Legion Post, the chapel went to the Martha's Vineyard Hospital, where it continues to serve its religious function.)

The *Gazette* also successfully campaigned against the demolition of stone walls undulating at the edges of Chilmark and West Tisbury fields like the tail of a dragon, saving them from stone-crushers who planned to grind up the historic walls for surfacing highways.

Henry wrote the feisty editorials and most of the letters to politicians enlisting their help in preserving the Vineyard, and spoke out eloquently at town meetings. But in their splendidly symbiotic relationship, it was Betty who pushed him. Rarely she would consider some conservation matter in her own "Things Insular" column, but she recognized that

Captain Matrix ("Matsy") and his owners outside the *Gazette* office on a warm spring day. *Courtesy of the* Vineyard Gazette

most of the attention went to her husband's writing and his sunnier personality. And she was immensely proud of him, though she criticized and carped.

One of her own conservation outcries was written in 1959, as more and more houses began to appear on island hillsides. She grieved over the boulders they were supplanting on the Chilmark hills. "Who thinks twice," she wrote, "before forcing a new road through the still nearly primeval growth in some sections of the Island? Who pauses for a rock? Who hesitates before putting a shovel—probably a power shovel—into a kame?" She called upon the Dukes County Historical Society to do something about it.

The affection for trees inspired by the Pine Knob woods led, time after time, to Betty's campaigns to prevent the felling of island trees. In 1962 when hotelkeeper George C. Woods was requesting selectmen's permission to cut down eight trees in the heart of Vineyard Haven to make way for a parking lot, Betty wrote in "Things Insular" of how the loss of those elms and maples would only "add to the desolation of what was once a beautiful town. . . . If their lives are spared, they will guarantee to offer leafy shade and relief from the sun's rays . . . as well as to disguise the commercialism in the heart of the old town." She pleaded, "There is still time to save them, even at this eleventh hour, if you attend the public hearing on the premises tomorrow morning at 10:30." Townspeople responded to her pleas, and the Tisbury selectmen voted against the parking lot plan.

Similarly, the Houghs rallied to the defense of a Scotch elm that gracefully shaded South Water Street. The homeowner on whose property it grew insisted that the tree was diseased and that its branches, rubbing her house, were causing damage, and she wanted it removed. The tree warden found that its illness could be easily cured by feeding and spraying, and the town took it upon itself to do both—as well cutting the offending branches. The elm's canopy shielded passersby from the summer sun for two more years; then the homeowner, in violation of the state shade tree law, had it cut down anyway. Betty's anger could not be assuaged. The homeowner's letter of explanation (sent to Henry, not Betty) fairly trembled on the page with apologies about broken tree limbs, and wet leaves on the sidewalk causing a lawsuit if someone slipped on them. Otherwise, of course, she wrote defensively, she would never have considered removing the tree (and added a shy inquiry after Betty's health).

Betty and Henry were usually in agreement with the Martha's Vineyard Garden Club on conservation issues. However, in 1951, Betty vented her wrath on Garden Club president Mrs. Wilfred O. White over the club's support of the state's tree-topping policies. "It should be no surprise to you," Betty wrote in a letter, "to know that I am in favor of saving all trees on this Island no matter how warped or distorted they may be. A tree is a tree is a tree, and there I make my stand."

Animal lover that she was, Betty was constantly fighting hunting interests. Not only was all Hough land posted to prohibit hunting, but Henry and Betty also tried to persuade others to do the same. In 1954, Betty's anguish was evident in a letter to Chilmark landowner Dr. Robert N. Ganz, as she hoped to persuade him to close his more than four hundred acres of woods and fields to hunters. "For more than a year," Betty wrote, "I have been agitating against the slaughter of fawns. The state's headquarters of the SPCA promised to carry the ball on this, but the results have been disappointing. For instance, when a few farmers, sportsmen and three officials of the State Division of Fish and Game conferred in our office at a meeting called by the SPCA representatives, Henry, Dr. Jones (the Foote Memorial Shelter veterinarian) and I found ourselves voices crying in the wilderness with all other voices raised in favor of striking down the deer—fawns and all, and the SPCA representatives remaining silent. It was a dreadful experience."

"Betty was the conscience of the *Gazette*," Henry always said. In their first year at the paper, she even banned patent medicine advertising, then an economic mainstay of newspapers.

The advocates of conservation and preservation didn't always win, of course. A fire tower was erected in the Indian Hill woods despite *Gazette* protests. Although zoning was enacted in Oak Bluffs in 1948 (regulating lot size, setbacks, the location of business districts, and so forth) it was not until twenty-one years later, Hough campaigning notwithstanding, that Henry and Betty's beloved Edgartown agreed to it. But the Hough philosophy, as Henry put it, was simply to meet the emergencies that arose, and, seizing the opportunity, to try to go ahead and pursue whatever appeared realizable.

Chapter 19

Of Books and Writing

Despite Henry Hough's dedication to crafting strong editorials to promote his causes, he and Betty never let island controversies keep him from his other writing. His quick mind was always teeming with ideas for novels and short stories; Betty was always eager to direct her keen editor's eye on his fiction. Between the publication of *Martha's Vineyard: Summer Resort* and *Country Editor*, Henry considered writing a detective story with the atmosphere (but not the plot) of the infamous Lizzie Borden murder case; the trial was held in New Bedford just before he was born. (Sunday School teacher Borden was accused of murdering her father and mother, but acquitted.) Henry was thinking of mother and son murderers who were so absorbed in their own life and relationship that they were completely merciless to the rest of the world. He also envisioned writing a series of small-town stories, including one set at a country newspaper. But then he went to South Africa, and began *That Lofty Sky* instead.

Another idea for a novel arose from his research for *Martha's Vineyard: Summer Resort*; he became intrigued with the singer Lillian Norton, granddaughter of an early Camp Meeting preacher. She went abroad to sing and, under the name Madame Nordica, gained renown as one of the world's great Wagnerian singers. She was the inspiration for the heroine of his fifth book, *All Things Are Yours*. Three years later came *Roosters Crow in Town,* his novel with a country newspaper theme. Woven into the plot were the amphibious forces which held maneuvers on the island during the war years. Next was *Long Anchorage,* a historical novel set in New Bedford, full of the waterfront smells of tar and seasoned timber that he remembered from his childhood, and the "brave houses and flowery gardens" Herman Melville once said were "harpooned and dragged up . . . from the sea."

Hough novels met with mixed reviews, usually polite but never ecstatic. The *Providence Journal*'s New Bedford–born critic Bradford F. Swan was not impressed with *Long Anchorage;*

Still, later that year, he was at work on a New England novel that he was calling *Far Out the Coils,* and his work on Thoreau fascinated him. And the next summer, their social life included stimulating cocktail and dinner parties in Vineyard literary circles, with the Goulds, the novelist I.A.R. Wylie, and actress Katharine Cornell and her husband Guthrie McClintic, a producer, director, and writer. But Henry was still concerned that his life would not be long enough to write all the books he had notes for. He always thought he could write in any spare moment, but now he was finding that wasn't the case; he could only write when heaven was "cooperative and willing." He feared he might not have time to finish what he was already writing, let alone start new ones "in the shrinking space of life."

In 1956 came more discouraging news. The publisher Scribner's rejected his novel *Far Out the Coils.* Oddly, that rejection made Hough rally, and he began a revision. Speedy writer that he was, under normal circumstances he could have revised the novel in three or four weeks, but Betty had broken an arm (the previous year she had broken the other arm), and he was swamped by his responsibilities at the *Gazette.* He finally managed a revision nonetheless, and the book was published by Random House two years later, under the title *The New England Story.* In it a young New Yorker goes to a New England town looking for information about a famous—but mysterious—nineteenth-century whaling captain. Henry was inspired to write it by his work on the book *Whaling Wives,* begun by West Tisbury poet and historian Emma Mayhew Whiting. After her death, he completed the unfinished book, rekindling his boyhood interest in whaling.

Meanwhile, he changed to a new literary agency, larger than Littauer's, with specialized departments. It was against his principles, he admitted, to support anything big and specialized, "yet I have only one life to live and there is a good deal to recommend the big agency." As he reflected on his literary output so far, he noted that his successful books were usually first greeted by agents and publishers "with contumely and loathing while the books and stories initially praised by writing scouts had, in the end, never been published."

The larger agency was Russell and Volkening; a deep and long-lasting friendship with Henry Volkening followed, as well as the successful publication of some half dozen books. It was Volkening who suggested that, with Hough's bent for whaling stories, he should try his hand at children's books; he wrote two, *Great Days of Whaling* and *Melville in the South Pacific.* In 1960 came his *Lament for a City,* a novel about a young, idealistic newspaperman in a thriving New England coastal city at the start of the twentieth century. The book recounted the fate of the city and the once courageous newspaper, and was based, of course, on the New Bedford Henry had known and his father's *New Bedford Evening Standard.* Again, reaction was mixed, and Betty wrote scathingly to negative reviewers.

In 1963, one more novel, *The Port,* dealt with the real estate development of a summer place by out-of-towners. Like all Henry's novels, it was dedicated to Betty but, by then, the world they shared was collapsing.

Chapter 20

"Your Veins Hold My Sap"

On a bright, sunlit September Sunday in 1961, like the September day in 1919 when Betty had first visited the island as a *New Bedford Evening Standard* reporter, the Houghs were invited to a birthday party by Edith G. Blake. Edith Blake covered the tennis and racing news of the Edgartown Yacht Club for the *Gazette*. Like the Houghs, she was devoted to animals; Henry later called her "the last of Betty's protégés."

In honor of Edie's birthday and the end of summer, Betty had put on a crisp new lavender dress—the first lavender dress she ever owned. But when the Houghs got to the boathouse where the party was to be held, no one was there. Betty, who always kept track of the couple's social events and of Henry's speaking engagements, had mixed up the day. That night, Betty suffered the first of what doctors called a series of strokes. When morning came, Henry took Betty to see a Boston neurologist. From then on, over the next four years, Betty Hough gradually failed. Some doctors surmised that she had Parkinson's disease; others that she was suffering from arteriosclerosis. She continued to go to the office, but often the copy she edited had to be quietly re-edited in the back shop. Edie Blake began covering the Martha's Vineyard Hospital's Edgartown Open House Tour instead of Betty, and taking photographs and writing interviews for the *Gazette*.

Meanwhile, as "small, annoying but unimportant quirks" were besetting her, the doctors told Henry they could see no cure and Betty's condition would simply worsen. Henry, heartsick, hoping to brighten his life companion's remaining years, suggested that Betty take some time off from the paper. "But the *Gazette* is the only thing that keeps me awake," she told him.

By the spring of 1963, though she still watched the cardinals outside the kitchen window and spotted the first evening grosbeak of the season, she could no longer read or write. As the doctors had said, her illness was irreversible.

"She was the fire that burned in the *Gazette*," Hough wrote to her old friend and bird-watching mentor, ornithologist Guy Emerson of Chilmark. "She was the one who always said what she thought and be damned by tact or policy. She was the one who showed instinctive good judgment in the causes that might be worth fighting for—and never yielded. . . . I want, as soon as possible, to sell the *Gazette*. For forty-three years, she and I have been together, sharing everything, and I do not intend to continue beyond this partnership. . . . I do not want to see her personal touch vanish by degrees and I have no wish to undertake what would be a late and anti-climactic career. . . . The *Gazette* must change, but it will not change with my help. Let fresh hands take hold and meet the new challenges. . . . I expect to earn a living by writing."

All the same, during Betty's illness, Henry took on much of her *Gazette* responsibility. Bill Roberts, Joe Allen, and Colbert Smith (a North Carolinian who joined the paper for

Betty Hough with last-minute corrections for Bill Roberts at his Linotype machine.
Photograph by Gretchen Van Tassel, courtesy of the Vineyard Gazette

"She was the fire that burned in the *Gazette*," Henry Hough said of Betty. *Courtesy of the* Vineyard Gazette

reporting and advertising in 1952, went to the Korean War in 1955, and returned to stay, becoming an editor) gave all their support, but Henry still was needed. However, as she became increasingly confined to the house, Betty needed him even more.

Peter and Jane Bunzel visited the Vineyard in the summer of 1963, before Bunzel, a *Life* magazine editor, moved from New York to Seattle, Washington. They wanted to see the godmother of two of their sons one last time. Fifteen years before, Betty had considered Bunzel, one of her *Gazette* interns, almost as her own son. She and Henry had offered him the *Gazette* as a present much as Henry's father had given it to them. But the Bunzels, at the time of the offer, already had a sizable family and knew the *Gazette* couldn't support them.

The brief Bunzel stay was a great relief to Henry; in this time of gradual loss, he needed old friends to share his sorrow. The Bunzels were a reassuring presence, too, on their outings around the island to the places Betty loved, such as Fish Hook and the Rogers house. Henry was afraid she might jump from the car—once she did, thinking she had seen the pony of her childhood in a field. Betty had always managed and harangued Henry, but deeply cared for him. During Betty's illness he was at his very best, friends said: calm, accepting, devoted, uncritical.

When Betty became totally bedridden, Henry hired day- and night-shift nurses for her. He would get up before 6 a.m. and walk their collie Lochinvar, take a quick trip to the office, and come back in time to help serve Betty's breakfast. Lochie was quick to return to his mistress's side, nuzzling her hand gently with his long nose. After breakfast, Henry went back to the *Gazette* until 12, then come home to help with Betty's lunch before his afternoon stint at the paper. In the evening, he and Betty and Lochie would be together as always—except that they were upstairs in the bedroom instead of downstairs in the big living room and Betty was no longer reading Willa Cather or Rudyard Kipling. Yet, "ill as she is," Henry wrote to Guy Emerson, "she is still Betty, and it shows in so many ways."

Thinking, perhaps, of what was soon to come, Henry remembered how Betty had insisted that all *Gazette* obituaries show an appreciation for what the deceased was like and what he or she meant to the community. "She always had . . . that element most lacking in modern journalism—heart," he said in his letter to Emerson.

"We never thought it would be like this for us. We had thought—or dreamed—that sometime far off, we would step out quietly together and turn the paper over to successors who loved the island, good English and so on," Henry wrote to William A. Caldwell, a New Jersey newspaper columnist and Edgartown seasonal visitor. And he reminisced about the past—how Betty saw the full moon taking up the whole width at the foot of Main Street and told him to write about it. He recalled how she would wake at night and make notes on a pad when she had an idea one of her reporters should write about. And, at the end of summer, "in a time we never thought would come—on a sunny Indian summer afternoon, she would say 'Let's get out of here.' And everyone would shut down and go into the sunshine and sweet autumn air."

What, Henry wondered, would happen to the *Gazette,* to him, to Martha's Vineyard without her?

Although they managed to save Sheriff's Meadow as a sanctuary when they created their foundation, they had also wanted to assure that Fish Hook would remain as it was. Virtually every spring, summer, and fall Sunday was spent there with Henry's father. While Henry and a dog walked in the woods, Betty had long talks on the Fish Hook porch with George Sr. The bond between Betty and her father-in-law was an especially strong one and, as he had aged, she always saw to his needs. As a birthday present one year, she connived with Alfred Hall, owner of the Edgartown movie theater, to put on a private showing of the circus film *The Greatest Show on Earth* for circus-loving "Pat," as George Sr. was known to his family and close friends. Winters, she made sure Pat was in Edgartown if he was not away on a cruise; sometimes he stayed with them or, if he rented an apartment, Betty made sure he would be safe when he was by himself. One winter when he was away on a cruise, she saw to it that his sons had electricity, heat, and running water installed at Fish Hook. When Pat returned, he grumbled that Betty must think he was in his dotage, but he enjoyed the new amenities, especially since they made entertaining easier. George Sr. never ceased to like having friends stop in for a blue martini (made with blue curaçao) and a few smoked oysters.

George Sr. died in 1955, leaving Fish Hook to his two sons. His property, in addition to the house, consisted of about a hundred acres of beech, oak, and maple woodlands, a brook, a swamp, a deep ravine, a bog, and a peat hole where ducks often found refuge. Almost a quarter of a mile of shore was just west of Cedar Tree Neck. Henry and Betty had often talked of preserving Fish Hook as a wildlife sanctuary. Since his brother had sons and grandchildren who also loved the property, Henry expected that he would have to buy his brother out. He and Betty had thought, in the mid-1960s, that this would cost $20,000.

Any money left after he had tended to Betty's needs should go to preserve Fish Hook and other natural areas of the Vineyard that were havens for wildlife. This, he felt, would be "at least a symbolical or vicarious reward for all her years of work on the Vineyard."

On June 20, 1965, Elizabeth Bowie Hough died. The day was bright and Edgartown's white picket fences and blue harbor waters shimmered in the sun. The previous Thursday was the last time Betty had spoken to him. "Hello, Henry," she had said with a slight smile. "I hadn't known then . . . that this was also 'Goodbye,'" he later wrote. Henry had worked that Monday morning, but he knew by the time he had finished his noontime cheese sandwich that he would not be returning to the *Gazette* that day. Shortly after Henry's lunch, the day nurse called Dr. Nevin to say that Betty's condition was critical.

Bob Nevin and Betty had often parried about this and that on her visits to his office. Because of foot problems, bouts with psychological malaise, and her series of broken bones, she often had doctor's appointments on Friday afternoons after the paper came out. Weary from the long work week, she would scold the good-natured doctor about his duck hunting and complain about what was wrong with him, medicine in general, and the island. Nevin would tell her she was neurotic, and she would retort that it took one to know one. He would tell her she was too confrontational and she would get up, walk out, and not speak to him for weeks afterwards. Then some event involving a Nevin or a Hough dog—such as Lochinvar's encounter with Nevin's Labrador—would mean all was forgiven. The Nevins also once had a dog named Maggie; after a kitchen fire at their house, Betty's *Gazette* headline read "Fire in Nevin Kitchen, Maggie Escapes." When the Nevins' golden retriever, Nutmeg, killed their children's two pet rabbits, Betty's gentle story about it in the *Gazette* soothed the sorrowing Nevin youngsters.

Bob Nevin came to the house that sparkling June afternoon, felt Betty's pulse, and told Henry quietly there was nothing further he could do. By mid-afternoon, Betty had died. Back at the *Gazette* office, they knew, too—the pendulum clock in the newsroom stopped.

Betty had once given Henry a few lines from "The Anniversary," a poem by Amy Lowell:

> You wrong me, saying:
> One death will not kill us both.
> Your veins hold my sap.

For forty-five years, those lines had described their relationship. "She and I have been together, sharing everything," Henry wrote to a friend, and speculated about how he could go on without her.

The following Friday, the front page of the *Gazette's* annual Directory Edition, which heralded the arrival of summer, was dedicated to Elizabeth Bowie Hough. The headline over her obituary read "Of All Who Loved the Gazette, She Loved It Best." The article ended, "She is survived by her husband, her brother, her newspaper and her collie dog."

Tributes to her came from *Gazette* colleagues, neighbors, friends, and fellow journalists from all over the nation. Bill Roberts remembered how her "clear, melodic, spirited" whistling of the hymn "Fight the good fight with all thy might" was often heard in the *Gazette* newsroom. He wrote of her typewriter pounding out countless columns for preservation of roadsides, trees, and other natural resources. "If what she sought at the moment was not especially popular, no matter. The fight was joined and her spirit was unflagging."

Twenty-six-year-old apprentice printer Jon Sawyer recalled that when she was against something she was "as strong as the stormy sea," but otherwise her disposition was "as gentle as a summer breeze." He said he would never forget "her bright blue eyes and snow white hair and pink, pink cheeks."

"She was a great and able newspaperwoman, and was deeply respected in her trade," an editorial column in the *Cape Codder* in neighboring Orleans said. "She had a curiosity that never dimmed about people and the world they lived in. She had compassion for living things, and she had a bite about her, too, although when she fought in her newspaper, it was a fair fight, a tasteful fight."

The *Amityville Record* in Amityville, Long Island, noted that she had helped make the *Gazette* "not just one of the nation's great weeklies, but one of the nation's great newspapers."

Even though in Betty's lifetime it was Henry who garnered most of the accolades for the *Gazette* (Betty at least received a Fiftieth Award Medal from Columbia for accomplishment), in death, even her candor was heralded. "When her heart spoke, she never held it back with timidity or cautions of prudence," one admirer wrote. "Henry and Betty were one person," Peter Bunzel said. "She was constantly pushing him to be strong and to Hell with what people thought." She was lauded as a crusader who waged war on injustices of every sort.

For months, Henry could not accept his loss. He saw little future without Betty. However, he also wanted to honor her memory, as he had written to Guy Emerson, by doing what she would have wanted—saving Fish Hook and, later, Cedar Tree Neck. But first he must find the right owners for the *Gazette*.

Chapter 21

Sale of the *Gazette*

Even before Betty's illness, Henry and Betty had pondered what they would do some day with the *Gazette*. After they had offered it to Peter Bunzel, they tried to sell it to another of their former summer reporters, Howard Young, who was prospering in a career in journalism in Washington. But it was not the right time in his life, either, for such a radical job change. The Houghs also explored whether their alma mater, the Columbia School of Journalism, might be interested in buying the *Gazette* as a training ground for aspiring reporters, but nothing came of their inquiry, and they had not pressed the issue. They felt they had plenty of time; Betty liked being an editor and Henry, since the 1950s, had been free of most *Gazette* responsibilities so he could write his books.

But after Betty was gone, Henry's own writing was out of the question unless he found a buyer for the paper. Moreover, the new owner had to share the same beliefs and journalistic ideals as his and Betty's, and the same devotion to the island.

Just as the Houghs together had approached former summer reporters Bunzel and Young about taking over the *Gazette*, now Henry, alone, sought out still another. William Jordan had gone on from the *Gazette* to the *New York Times* as the Moscow correspondent. He then served as United States ambassador to the Soviet Union and to Panama, but retained his island ties and Chilmark summer house. Although Bill Jordan did not see a future for himself at the *Gazette*, he ultimately introduced Henry to the right buyer.

Soon after word got out that Betty was ill, several prospective purchasers made inquiries. A group of *New York Times* editors nearing retirement—and with Vineyard summer homes—expressed interest in buying the paper together, keeping Colbert Smith as its editor, temporarily, at least. Henry was not interested in their offer, however, on the grounds that a committee could not edit a newspaper. Bill Caldwell, about to retire from

New Jersey's *Bergen Record,* wrote for financial particulars. New Jersey philanthropist Fairleigh S. Dickinson Jr., a lifelong Edgartown summer resident and former commodore of the Edgartown Yacht Club, asked Edgartown insider Bob Carroll if he knew what Henry was asking for the paper.

But the most serious prospect, as far as Henry was concerned, was Michael J. Straight, the former editor and publisher of the weekly journal of opinion the *New Republic.* Straight's Vineyard links went back to an aunt with a home at Indian Hill; he had summered on Chappaquiddick and at Lambert's Cove before buying a house on Quitsa Pond in Chilmark. A decade earlier, in 1965, Straight established the Vineyard Conservation Society with Roger Baldwin and Dr. Leona Baumgartner, public health commissioner for the city of New York, who also had a Chilmark house. Straight had both the editorial credentials and the desire to preserve the island essential to Henry and Betty for their successor.

Henry outlined the finances for him. The *Gazette* had never attained a gross business income of $100,000, but it had been well above $90,000, he wrote to Straight in 1963, when he knew Betty's death was only a matter of time. Henry pointed out frankly that they had never taken more than $16,000 a year from the paper between them. With other income— principally from his writing—the two of them made a total of about $20,000 a year. A little wistfully he added, "So we have not denied ourselves much of anything that we really want- ed, though those things that we vetoed when we were younger are gone forever." He also would not interfere in any way with a new owner of the *Gazette,* he said, but hoped any changes wouldn't be toward conformity or false sophistication.

He was uncertain of what price to ask, but in a letter to Pen Dudley he said he thought Straight would be willing to pay about $100,000. "A hundred thousand, even with taxes out, represents a great deal of money from my standpoint. . . . It is unlikely that I will ever leave the Vineyard again since I detest travel. There's no entertainment any city can offer that could approximate what Betty and I have had in the past.

"Yet when it comes to putting a price on the privation and hardship Betty and I have invested in the *Gazette . . .* I am not willing it should be held cheaply."

To Dudley, Hough reiterated his thoughts to Straight about hoping the *Gazette* would not change toward conformity, but added that he would not want a buyer to try to imitate the paper as it had existed under the Houghs either.

But as Betty's condition worsened, and his burden of work both at home and at the *Gazette* increased, Hough put aside all thoughts of the sale of the paper.

Then, the summer Betty died, Henry had a chance meeting with James B. Reston, the Scottish-born *New York Times* columnist who was moving from the post of bureau chief of the *Times* in Washington to be executive editor in New York City. Scotty Reston's first visit to the Vineyard was a retreat from city hubbub to work on a book of reminiscences, *Sketches in the Sand.*

In the summer of 1963, James B. ("Scotty") Reston of the *New York Times* with his wife, Sally, and their son Jim visited Martha's Vineyard for the first time.
Copyright Alfred Eisenstaedt

He and his wife Sally rented a house in Chilmark for part of the summer. One evening, Bill Jordan invited them to his house to meet some of their Chilmark neighbors and Jordan's old boss, Henry Beetle Hough.

"Henry was a tough, gutsy old fellow," Reston later recalled, "and we got on very well. We found a quiet corner where the two of us could talk, and Henry told me that he was very worried about the *Gazette*." Now that he was seventy, and Betty was gone, he didn't know how much longer he could keep up with the demands of the paper, Henry told Reston. But since they had spent so much of their lives with it, even though he wanted to sell, he didn't want to sell out. He felt an obligation to find a successor who would be committed to the welfare of the island. When the cocktail party broke up, each expressed pleasure at having met the other and Scotty returned to his executive editor's position at the *Times*.

Two years later, with no move from Straight, Henry was absolutely certain he wanted to sell. He was at last beginning to feel enough like his old self to want to return to book writing. He thought again of Scotty Reston and sent him an inquiring letter.

"When a door like that opens," Reston said, "you should walk through it." So the fifty-eight-year-old *New York Times* editor wrote back that he knew of a "perky, middle-aged Scot, Reston, by name . . . who might like to buy the *Vineyard Gazette*. He has some experience reporting on politics and even foreign affairs, but he is getting to the point where he is more interested in reporting on life than anything else." In addition, Reston wrote, he had three writing sons. The eldest, Richard, started out as a reporter with United Press International and then moved on to the *Los Angeles Times* and was then foreign correspondent and bureau chief in Moscow. James Jr. briefly worked for the *Chicago Daily News* and while still in Army Intelligence in Hawaii had begun a novel. The youngest son, Tom, an undergraduate at Harvard, was also looking forward to a career in journalism. Since Henry wanted continuity for his paper, the idea of an upcoming generation of Restons who were writers was extremely appealing.

By now, Henry was asking $150,000 for the paper. When the transaction with James and Sally Reston was completed in March of 1968, his payment was $101,490, plus $27,000 not to compete by starting another paper for five years. He also agreed to keep writing the editorials, for which he would be paid. Henry was satisfied with this arrangement; he was not being shortchanged, and he was certain Betty would have approved of Scotty Reston as a buyer.

Even though Reston was a newcomer to the intimate Vineyard world, and his experience was international, he seemed to have a feeling for nature. He had a country place in rural Virginia where he fished in Blue Ridge Mountain streams, tried to make vegetables grow in his garden, and happily rode the tractor-mower as he cut his fields. When he was a boy, he loved long walks over the Scottish moors with his father. Sally Reston came from Sycamore, Illinois, a little town named after, and famous for, the sycamore trees bordering its river. Like Betty, Sally believed trees should be saved.

Scotty Reston, a Pulitzer Prize winner twice, had interviewed presidents, prime ministers, and kings for the *New York Times*, yet remained unpretentious and forthright. Both liberals, Henry and Scotty were also politically attuned. The Houghs were *New York Times* readers and had applauded Scotty Reston's opinions in his columns.

In 1968, however, no Reston son was ready to move to Martha's Vineyard and become a country editor. Dick (except for the caviar to which he was allergic) was enjoying his Moscow post, Jim was involved in his writing, and Tom planned to travel around the world after Harvard.

Although Henry wanted to be free of responsibility for the paper now that a new owner was in charge, he agreed to keep on writing its editorials and advising the staff for a while longer. Colbert Smith still ran the office as assistant editor, as he had since 1961; Joe Allen continued, unflagging, as reporter and ad-getter even at seventy-two; and Edie Blake was doing more and more writing and photography.

However, Henry could not let up; he had more battles to wage. In 1969, Northeast Airlines, with a route between New York and the island, announced that all Vineyard flights would be jet service only, requiring the extension of the runway. A glide path for planes was also necessary, according to the Federal Aviation Administration. To accommodate this expansion, some sixty-five acres of oaks and pines in the abutting state forest would have to be felled. County commissioners regarded the expansion as an economic necessity and requested an easement to allow the tree-cutting. The FAA also planned to lower a section of the road beside the airport as a safety measure.

Angry island residents, opposed to the destruction of the woodland and the altering of an old country road, formed a Concerned Citizens organization to fight the federal demand. Henry Hough was asked to join its board of directors. With Betty's combative spirit and her love of the Vineyard's trees "no matter how warped or distorted they may be" as his inspiration, Henry spoke out against the project at the FAA hearing. He asked whether "the destiny of this Island, its way of life, its values . . . are to be handed over to transportation lines and government agencies in which we have no representation."

Though Henry had dreamed that selling the paper would mark a change in his life, and at last he would be totally free to write, it was not to be. With Betty's death, a new Henry emerged. He always had been a formidable opponent of the destruction of the wild green Vineyard they both loved. But often Betty spearheaded their campaigns, goading him into taking the roles he was better suited for: serving on public boards, persuading officials in high places with his diplomacy, swaying public opinion with his editorials. Now, with the *Gazette* sold, the responsibility as the Vineyard's caretaker was no longer his, but Betty would not have wanted him to give up just yet. The Restons were newcomers to the Vineyard and absentee owners of the paper. Henry was still called to be the keeper of the Vineyard, and he gallantly accepted the position. (His enemies, of course, still attacked him as a "hypocrite with blinders on" who brought people to the island with the books he wrote, only to complain when locals sold land to them and pristine woods and fields became house lots.)

The fight to save the forest went on for the next two years; Henry and the Concerned Citizens speculated that the federal government wanted a jet airport on the island not to serve the public but for its own purposes. Although the Concerned Citizens managed to get a ruling from the State Supreme Court that would have saved the trees, they seemed doomed anyway when the legislature passed a bill allowing the conversion of the forest to a use other than tree-growing. The victory Henry and fellow conservationists won this time—the first since Betty's death—was a compromise. Although twenty-five acres of forest were saved, the road lost its picturesque embankments. As for Northeast Airlines, after one summer, they ended their Vineyard flights.

Meanwhile, Colbert Smith returned to the South to edit a weekly newspaper in Kentucky. As a result, an impatient Henry found himself spending more time than he liked on day-to-day affairs at the *Gazette*. Even though the staff had expanded—with two retired newspapermen, Caldwell from the *Bergen Record* (who had decided not to buy the paper himself) and Donal MacPhee from the *Springfield Republican,* plus a full-time young reporter and a new managing editor from the *New York Times*—Henry went into the office each day. Except on press days, he tried to write at home mornings, his habit from his years with Betty, but he couldn't always. He missed her in the big house they had built and the garden he had planted for her. He missed her advice—albeit so often sharp—her inspiration, and her editing skills.

Then, in 1972, came another great personal blow. Back-shop superintendent Bill Roberts succumbed to cancer. For forty-seven years, Bill Roberts of the bow ties and impeccable appearance—belying the name "black gang"—not only ran the *Gazette's* back shop, but also filled in as editor when necessary. (He was left in charge while Henry and Betty worked in New York.) He and the Houghs were the paper's only shareholders. The collaboration formed in the 1920s "just as solidly as an old-fashioned blood compact" between Henry and Betty, Bill, and Joe Allen had now lost two of its beloved members. Sitting below the stained glass window of the Toilers of the Sea in Edgartown's St. Andrew's Church during Bill's funeral, Henry Hough was once again in dark sadness.

Chapter 22

The Vineyard Discovered

Henry was increasingly worried about the Vineyard; the airport expansion was only one issue. Just four years after Betty's death, Senator Edward M. Kennedy's car plunged off the Dike Bridge on Edgartown's neighboring island of Chappaquiddick and the senator's companion, Mary Jo Kopechne, was drowned. Notoriety had come to Martha's Vineyard.

Henry and Lochinvar had just left the *Gazette* office that sunny Saturday morning in July 1969 and were headed home when Henry learned of the tragedy. Suddenly he, Colbert Smith, and Scotty Reston, spending the weekend on the Vineyard, were all reporters again. Reston hurried to the police station to intercept Kennedy and talk with him. That effort failed, but nonetheless Reston was soon typing up a story for the Sunday *New York Times* front page. Sally Reston took inserts and additions and telephoned them to the *Times*. To a *Times* writer in Philadelphia, Henry read Kennedy's statement to the police.

Immediately, the island was flooded with reporters and photographers from all over the nation and from Rome, Toronto, London, Australia. Television cameras and crews impeded traffic on Main Street for weeks as the case continued. After Kennedy was found guilty of leaving the scene of an accident by District Court Judge James A. Boyle, reporters and photographers left, only to return in September, when an inquest into the death was held. When they were not covering the court case, reporters roamed the island in search of other stories to write; soon Chappaquiddick and Martha's Vineyard were household words everywhere. During this time writer Vance Packard, who had a Chappaquiddick home, gave his name and address to an off-island store so something could be mailed to him; the clerk taking the order asked for a spelling. Packard began spelling Chappaquiddick. "No, not that," the clerk interrupted. "Of course I know how to spell that. How do you spell Packard?"

Five years later, Martha's Vineyard was the site for the filming of Steven Spielberg's action thriller *Jaws*. Islanders of all ages—Dr. Bob Nevin among them—were hired to play such roles as medical examiner and escapees from the rapacious shark. The beach Betty Hough and Joseph A. Sylvia had persuaded the state to buy a few years earlier became the shark's playground.

The newspaper and magazine articles covering these events highlighted the island on the tourist map. It became a destination, in particular, for movie buffs wanting to see where *Jaws* had "happened," and for macabre day-trippers eager to gawk at the Dike Bridge. Henry decried how the bridge had turned into a tourist attraction, with visitors posing for snapshots on it and even whittling off pieces for souvenirs.

Then the off-island developers arrived. Vineyard farmland, by then not particularly productive, began to be offered for sale. In 1963, two Boston dentists, Moses and Alvin Strock, had acquired sizable tracts of property: the Island Country Club in Oak Bluffs, consisting of a golf course and clubhouse; and several hundred adjacent acres of old farms on pretty Sengekontacket Pond. Here the Indian princess Ahoma (also called Alice), daughter of the sachem of Sengekontacket, was courted by white settler Joseph Daggett, forebear of the North Shore Daggetts of Henry's childhood. Next, the Strocks bought land in the town of Gay Head and a section of Edgartown's South Beach, stating they wanted to preserve the "natural flavor" of the island in any future developing. Noting the island's sudden

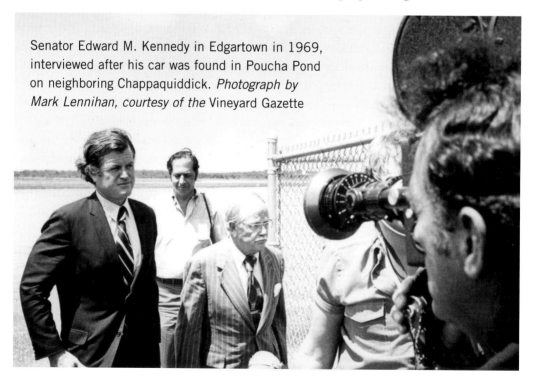

Senator Edward M. Kennedy in Edgartown in 1969, interviewed after his car was found in Poucha Pond on neighboring Chappaquiddick. *Photograph by Mark Lennihan, courtesy of the* Vineyard Gazette

Edgartown's Main Street became a movie set when Steven Spielberg's film *Jaws* was filmed on Martha's Vineyard. *Photograph by Edith G. Blake*

increase in popularity, they emphasized they would seek to prevent the creation of small-tract subdivisions. To this end, presumably, they bought parcels of pastureland on West Tisbury's Great Plains and of wooded land on the Middle Road in Chilmark. Then they enlarged their holdings with purchases in Oak Bluffs and Vineyard Haven.

At first, Henry viewed their purchases sanguinely; Alvin Strock had written warm letters about his family's love of the island. But as more and more island land became Strock land, Henry began to have second thoughts. By 1974, when the Vineyard had become a "hot" vacation destination, the Strocks were proposing an 867-lot subdivision on 507 acres. Henry's opinion changed: their development plan, he wrote, represented an intensity of land use greater than the island had ever known. "The Strock plan uses phrases such as 'cluster zoning' and 'greenbelts' to rationalize or justify a development. . . . The proposed subdivision of the beautiful slopes of Sengekontacket Pond . . . has implications for the whole Island, in congestion on the ferries, crowding in the towns, on the highways, use of Island facilities. . . . Here is, very clearly, the greatest threat so far to the Island's rural environment," Henry editorialized in 1974.

Meanwhile, mornings when the *Gazette's* Florence Brown was collecting real estate transaction news at the Dukes County Registry of Deeds in Edgartown's red-brick courthouse, she would see savvy developers leafing through the fat volumes of deeds looking for "forgotten" acreage that faraway heirs, unaware of the increasing value of Vineyard land, might be enticed to sell for low prices. Other property became available as towns raised taxes that owners were unable or unwilling to pay. In 1971, William H. Brine Jr. of Weston and Edgartown bought 229 West Tisbury acres from the property's Cleveland, Ohio, owner when the taxes increased seven-fold. Within a year after Brine and his associate, John Black of Edgartown (one of the delvers in the registry records) had paid $20,000 for the acreage, they resold it for $229,000 to developer Benjamin J. Boldt of Lexington, Massachusetts. Boldt announced his intention to construct seventy-five homes on the land; less population density, he happily commented, than in Beverly Hills, California, with its multimillion-dollar estates. "I'm going to have restrictive covenants on architecture so there'll be that horsey farm look all the way through, and no cutting up of property into small lots," he added. Originally in real estate in Oregon, Boldt became interested in island property on a summer visit to Edgartown a few years earlier. Before his enthusiasm for dealing in Vineyard real estate ended, Boldt bought and sold about 1,700 island acres, and also owned an airfield in Oak Bluffs and two hotels.

In 1971, in 107.2 acres of pine and oak woods he purchased near Vineyard Haven's pristine Lake Tashmoo, Joseph Chira of Rye, New York, was hoping to install 150 families. "Tashmoo is a fragile resource of importance to the whole Island," Henry wrote, worried. "The environmental impact of so large a new community would be too great for soil or water or the character of the region and its present economic level to sustain."

In Chilmark, West Tisbury, and Edgartown, former New York book publisher Nicholas Freydberg bought land and historic houses, including 450 Edgartown acres on quiet little Oyster and Watcha ponds. This land once belonged to Henry's childhood friend George Flynn. Freydberg emphasized that he was a land preservationist and sold only in large tracts. Among his buyers were such luminaries as the former secretary of defense Robert S. McNamara and former secretary of state Cyrus Vance, both regarding the island as their retreat from grave national and international concerns. Freydberg's Oyster-Watcha tracts, perched beside the ponds, were fifteen acres that could not be subdivided. Henry looked on Freydberg more as a land rescuer than a developer, and they became fast friends; Henry turned to Freydberg when he heard of land like Flynn's he knew should be preserved.

Not only off-island developers, but locals, as well, laid plans to profit from their land. Edgartown real estate developer Leo P. Convery sought to rezone a stretch at the bridge to Vineyard Haven as a business district so sixty residence units could be constructed on a five-acre sandspit at the edge of the harbor.

As development continued unabated, the island's county commission (three elected representatives overseeing regional government) sought federal funding for a study of the Vineyard's natural resources and its accelerated population and building growth. The commission hoped to identify potential problems so they could be avoided. (In 1971 there was one housing start a day; a year later, two a day.) Henry, in his editorial endorsement of the commissioners' request, had noted that overcrowding of the Vineyard could "extinguish our sense of spaciousness and sanctuary. And that could mean the end, in a realistic sense . . . of our insularity." He urged that the study be made before the situation worsened. Henry remembered when he and Betty made the Vineyard their home because of its security and insularity, now, clearly, threatened.

In company with the Concerned Citizens, the *Gazette* demanded the banning of big diesel tour buses: their fumes polluted the fresh sea air and their weight was destroying rural up-island roads. A nineteen-acre trailer park became the center of another battle; Henry, who contributed $500 to a fund to stop it, wearily asked if the island's new population pressures would "shape it into conformity with the blighted mainland." Control of the island's future, he felt, was falling into the hands of entrepreneurial strangers with quick-and-easy profit motives and no consideration for the island's welfare.

The 1971 Metcalf and Eddy report by a Boston engineering firm described Martha's Vineyard as "one of the few bastions of rural environmental splendor along the eastern coastline of the United States," but noted several problems: overpopulation and congestion on the island's main roads at peak traffic periods, damage to the dunes and heathlands of Gay Head by too many people trampling on them, salt water intrusion in Katama, noise and air pollution around the airport, septic tank and cesspool failures, and dangerous coliform counts in some island waters. The report offered several solutions, and in its first draft (which was rejected by the Dukes County Commission) warned that if its recommendations were not implemented by 1975, the Vineyard "will not only have been fully raped by the despoilers, but also will have contracted environmental terminal cancer." Henry, meanwhile, pleaded for zoning, historic preservation districts, conservation areas, limits to the influx of tourists. He urged the Steamship Authority to consider the well-being of the island rather than increasing the number of boat runs to bring more visitors. He suggested that Vineyarders selling land for development reflect on the fate of island landscapes and of wildlife as natural habitats disappeared.

Henry Hough was now in his seventies, but he was still vigorous. He had never ceased his walks through Sheriff's Meadow at sunrise with Lochinvar or his successor Graham. They still stepped briskly along the path encircling the old ice pond, cut through the Edgartown Yacht Club Tennis Club grounds to Pease's Point Way, passed the Greek Revival houses Henry and Betty had admired and longed for in their young days, crossed North Water Street and took the causeway to the Edgartown Lighthouse. Then they headed up Main Street to greet fellow early risers—man and dog—before going to the *Gazette* office. Often at midday, even into November, Henry would go for a quick swim in the inner or outer harbor.

At seventy-five in 1971, Henry was the oldest man to finish the ten-mile Foot-It-For-Felix foot race for the benefit of the Felix Neck Wildlife Sanctuary, one of his favorite pieces of land. He had been instrumental in persuading George Moffett Jr. to turn the 210 acres of flowing fields and hills, sparkling ponds and tidal marshes into a wildlife sanctuary. Developers were determined to persuade Walter Smith Jr. to sell them his family's old Felix Neck Farm when Moffett, long an Edgartown yachtsman and seasonal resident, had

Conservationist Anne Hale and
two young naturalists enjoy
"Fern and Feather" day camp
in the early days of the
Felix Neck sanctuary.
*Courtesy of Felix Neck
Library Archives*

learned of it. A conservationist as well, Moffett purchased the property to keep it out of a developer's hands, though he wasn't sure what he would do with it. One cold gray autumn afternoon he toured the land with Tom Hale, owner of the shipyard where his boat was hauled each winter, and his wife, Anne, a landscape architect and conservationist. The Hales' black Labrador retriever bounded through the tall grass after rabbits while the conservationists surveyed the woodlands and marshes, a haven for muskrats, otters, and box and spotted turtles. Anne Hale urged Moffett to turn the property into a wildlife sanctuary where children could learn about nature.

Moffett turned to Henry for further advice. Henry joined the sanctuary's first board of directors, which would meet outdoors on the old farmland, sitting on telephone company cable spools along with Hoot, a great horned owl and sanctuary mascot. Looking out over those fields above Sengekontacket Pond, Henry would consider with satisfaction the great expanse of land that the right combination of thoughtful people had kept from becoming a "suburban subdivision."

Meanwhile, Henry was still writing. In 1971, *Tuesday Will Be Different: Letters from Sheriff's Lane* appeared, a rueful and sometimes crochety book. One of these letters, all expressly written for the book, complained directly to Governor Francis Sargent about widening Vineyard roads into highways, a matter Henry had often editorialized against. In another, he wrote to FAA hearing officer Martin J. White decrying the airport runway extension. A letter to the President of the United States warned about DDT air pollution and SST (supersonic transport) sound pollution. Declining an invitation to share Thanksgiving turkey with his brother's family, he mourned the commercialism destroying the holiday. He wrote about the Dike Bridge and Senator Kennedy.

Soon, Ted Kennedy would play a major role on the Vineyard again, leading Henry to the most challenging—and most divisive—confrontation of his life.

Chapter 23

The Birth of the Kennedy Bill

One warm late summer night in 1971, Henry and Lochinvar had just come home from a stroll under the Milky Way when the telephone rang. Henry hurried into the kitchen to answer it, a little concerned; he was not accustomed to late-night calls. At the other end of the line was poet-activist Rose Styron, wife of Pulitzer Prize–winning novelist William Styron and a longtime Vineyard Haven seasonal resident. She apologized for the time of the call, but said Ted Kennedy was at her house. He had sailed over from Hyannisport and they had talked much of the afternoon on the Styrons' spacious lawn above Vineyard Haven harbor.

Now Kennedy wanted to tell Henry what he was thinking. When the senator got on the phone, he explained how he hoped to do something to protect the greatly endangered natural resources and character of the Vineyard and of Nantucket. He would be willing to "take considerable heat" in the cause of the islands, said the senator, even though he was endlessly attacked on the Vineyard after the incident at Chappaquiddick.

The following April, true to his word, Kennedy introduced his bill to preserve and conserve the islands of Nantucket Sound because of their unique scenic, ecological, scientific, historical, and recreational values. The bill was described as a working paper to be developed with state and local governments and private groups. Unfortunately, as Henry learned, neither Senator Edward W. Brooke, who had an Oak Bluffs home, nor elected officials of the Vineyard or Nantucket had been informed of Ted Kennedy's intentions. Instead, the bill was introduced to Vineyard locals at a press conference at the Martha's Vineyard Shipyard by Tom and Anne Hale. The Hales had moved to the Vineyard from Boston's North Shore, and knew from their experience there the importance of controlling the development of charming, inviting places. But since they were, in Vineyard parlance, off-islanders, local officials were enraged and insulted that their opinions and input had not been sought first. The proposed bill, after all, dealt with Vineyarders' welfare, yet was being developed by people from "away." The high-handed way the bill was introduced, Henry always said, was "disastrous."

Angriest of all was Harbor View Hotel owner Robert J. Carroll, former Edgartown selectman and president of the Martha's Vineyard Chamber of Commerce, restaurateur, and real estate developer. He would be the most powerful opponent of Ted Kennedy's Islands Trust Bill, telling Vineyarders the bill was the "work of people who think they are intellectually and socially superior." Reminiscing about his Edgartown youth, egalitarian Carroll always liked to recount how he was brought up in a tenement just across from the South Summer Street house that became the *Vineyard Gazette* building.

Rumor had it that hurt feelings played a part in Carroll's antagonism to the bill. In 1952, when Jack Kennedy was running for the U.S. Senate, he sent his younger brother, Ted, to Edgartown to make friends for him. One of them was Bob Carroll, then chairman of the Edgartown Democratic Town Committee. Ted Kennedy would even occasionally hitch rides to the Cape on the plane Bob Carroll owned and proudly piloted. After the tragedy on Chappaquiddick, Carroll had flown the senator back to Hyannis.

In 1971, islanders gathered to hear Senator Edward M. Kennedy explain his Nantucket Sound Islands Trust Bill, designed to save Martha's Vineyard and Nantucket from overdevelopment. *Photograph by Peter Simon, courtesy of the* Vineyard Gazette

Ted Kennedy's failure to let his Democratic flying pal in on his secret was, Henry Hough felt, significant for the Islands Trust Bill's undoing. Bridling at the slight and eager, in any case, to see real estate deals prosper on Martha's Vineyard, Bob Carroll used all his political skills to organize Vineyarders against the legislation. Only two years had passed since the senator's car went off the bridge on Chappaquiddick with Mary Jo Kopechne, and that memory was skillfully brought back.

An after-the-fact meeting with elected officials was finally called at the Harborside Inn in Edgartown, with former Kennedy aide K. Dun Gifford, entrusted by the senator to promote the bill. An able young lawyer—glib, handsome, and charming—and a Nantucket seasonal resident, he had seemed to Ted Kennedy the perfect choice to present his case.

Ted Kennedy took "considerable heat" as he sought support on the Vineyard for his Islands Trust legislation. *Photograph by Peter Simon, courtesy of the* Vineyard Gazette

To Bob Carroll, however, Gifford's patrician looks and Harvard accent were anathema. Bumper stickers proclaiming "Island Trust for the Upper Crust" were soon distributed. The Harborside Inn gathering was followed by a public meeting to discuss the proposed legislation.

For the next four years, the residents of Martha's Vineyard and Nantucket opposed to the legislation, among them many wealthy landowners and people in the construction industry, maintained that the bill would give the federal government too much control over local affairs. Bill supporters, with Hough in the forefront, insisted just the opposite—that more federal oversight should be specified in the legislation.

The trust bill proposed that most Vineyard and Nantucket land of scenic value be placed under control of a federal and local trust board, with representation from the two islands (including nonprofit preservation groups) and from the Cape Cod town of Barnstable, the Department of the Interior, and the Environmental Protection Agency. The bill sought $10 million from the federal government to acquire and protect endangered land.

Land on the islands would be divided into four categories. The most endangered land would be dubbed Forever Wild. Structures already on this land (much of it was privately owned) would be bought by the federal government and removed; no new structures would be allowed. The other categories were Scenic Preservation and Town and County Planned Lands. On Scenic Preservation land, existing buildings could remain, but no additional construction would be allowed. Town and County Planned Lands would be under local jurisdiction. In addition, until the bill was in place, there would be a freeze on all new building.

Henry printed the text of the bill in the *Gazette,* along with a map showing proposed land categories and a report on the press conference at the boatyard. The next *Gazette* issue reported island reaction to the bill. Opponents objected to federal meddling in local affairs, feared the end of home rule, and challenged the freeze on construction as harmful to the building trades and, as a result, to the economy. The bill was too vague, too restrictive, and probably unconstitutional, they added, decrying its secretive introduction and saying it made a mockery of the legislative process. Wealthy summer people with large tracts of land near beaches feared that the public would have access to them across private lands. For example, Horace B.B. Robinson of New York and Chilmark, a former law partner of presidential candidate Thomas E. Dewey, said the bill would create public beaches, and roads would be built to them across private land lined "with big gas stations and fast food concessions." He felt the people who came to public beaches on bikes or buses for just a day would destroy the Vineyard's tradition as a stable seashore community. Chilmark selectman and contractor Herbert Hancock was in the forefront of those in the building trades against the bill, describing it as "socialistic." The All-Island Selectmen's Association, the

Chamber of Commerce, and the county commissioners all voiced their opposition. On the other hand, proponents of the bill regarded it as the island's last chance and felt its shortcomings could be amended.

For some weeks, the *Gazette* simply reported on the bill and the viewpoints of both proponents and opponents. Editorially, Hough bided his time about endorsing the bill because he knew everyone expected him to support it. He also admitted, privately, that he had some reservations about the introduced legislation. "If there had been a chance of keeping the Vineyard as it was ten years ago or five years ago, I would have thought the bill a terrible one," he said, "but today, with the prospect that awaits the Islands with certainty if nothing is done, I can see the bill as wonderful."

As the dialogue continued, the *Gazette* quietly informed readers what lay ahead without the bill. Referring to the dire predictions of the Metcalf and Eddy report, Henry warned that, as the island's population grew, ground water was at risk: developers were laying out new subdivisions daily with no concern for safe standards for water purity and sewage disposal. He also pointed out that if land speculation continued at the present rate, Vineyarders themselves would be forced out of the market.

Across the island, sides were taken. John Alley of West Tisbury helped organize a group called Vineyarders to Amend the Bill, while Bob Carroll established the Island Action Committee to defeat it. About a month after the bill's first mention on Martha's Vineyard, Henry decided it was time to endorse it, and called Scotty Reston to tell him. Though Reston was now the *Gazette*'s owner, he let Hough write editorially as he saw fit. However, the Islands Trust Bill was a major matter, and it involved Reston's bailiwick— Washington. Reston quickly acquiesced to Henry's decision; the front page *Gazette* editorial headline of May 26, 1972, read "The Kennedy Bill Must Be Enacted." Hough pointed out, however, that the bill should be amended to assure that even though building was slowed down, the island's carpenters and plumbers and electricians were not brought to ruin.

Referring to the island-wide division over the bill, he remarked, "The differences among us are not of good against evil or summer people against all-year people . . . they are basically of conservatives who would protect and hold as much of the Island heritage in its present form as possible, and of liberals who have a dedicated love of the Island and would take bold steps to save it."

Publicly, Henry Hough was at his best during the Kennedy Bill crisis. His quick mind could comprehend the complex legislative language. He was convinced the bill had to become law, if anything was to remain of the Vineyard he and Betty loved. As he faced down Bob Carroll and his Island Action Committee at public meetings, dinner parties, and on street corners, he was as fearless and outspoken as Betty would have been. Privately, however, Henry was typing out his despair in his upstairs study overlooking the sliver of blue pond and green vegetation that had meant so much to Betty. "At the moment there's a sickening tide against the Kennedy Bill—those old symbols and inflammatory phrases—'Take away our rights,' 'federal dictation,' 'ruin the livelihood of the building industry' and so on," he wrote to Howard Young. "The poor old Vineyard . . . I don't know how many more of these tense, emotional confrontations I can live through."

But Henry rallied to combat and, for the next four years, he devoted all his energy to the fight. He even set aside his creative writing.

In response to Hough's support of the Kennedy Bill, Bob Carroll's Island Action Committee asked *Gazette* advertisers to stop placing ads. Henry was also warned that the threat of the bill was making property owners sell their land to developers as soon as possible—the opposite of what he wanted—for fear, otherwise, the federal government would take it and they would lose all their rights to it. Then one night a fire started in the *Gazette*'s back shop. No culprit was ever found, and, happily, the sprinkler system put out the blaze, but many assumed that the fire was set by a bill opponent hoping to "get back" at Henry and the *Gazette*.

Two years after the bill's introduction, the governor of Massachusetts, at the urging of Carroll and other opponents of the Kennedy Bill, developed a conservation bill of his own. Henry didn't think much of it. On November 8, 1973, he wrote stingingly to Governor Sargent: "It happens that I am 77 years old today. This is really getting along, but at the rate things are going, I shall have ample time to write the obituary of Martha's Vineyard. . . . If you succeed in reviving the . . . State Bill . . . for the exploitation and development of the Vineyard, your part in the obituary will be a prominent one and I can write it well. . . . I am aware that this is an angry letter, but I have a right to be angry, for I have given my life to Martha's Vineyard, and I do not like those who would pillage the Island, no matter how sanctimoniously."

Hough criticized the Sargent Bill for failing to control the enormous number of people and automobiles coming to the islands. However, by the spring of 1974, the governor's bill was being considered by an island-wide referendum. In the end, after the bill's many revisions, Henry, too, endorsed it, when he had almost given up hope for the Kennedy Bill. He believed that the governor's bill, in its final form, gave local officials sufficient power to control building in areas needing preservation. But he still had greater faith in the Islands Trust Bill, which would provide federal funds for conservation, a clear necessity if fragile island land was to be saved. The federal and the state bills together—with federal monies supporting the state legislation—might be enough to preserve and protect the Vineyard, Hough felt.

Before the referendum, Henry informed *Gazette* readers that he no longer saw rivalry between the two bills and had high hopes for the enactment of both. The Kennedy Bill was, at the time, poised for introduction in Congress. When the referendum was held, the

Sargent Bill was endorsed by a two-to-one margin; then the state legislature passed it.

However, sadly for Henry and his beloved Vineyard, no such positive reception await-ed the trust bill, still being revised and pondered. Henry was cautiously exuberant when it passed by a voice vote in the Senate in 1975. But in June of the following year, a hearing on the bill was scheduled in Washington before the House Subcommittee on Parks and Recreation. For years Henry had not ventured off-island any farther than Boston for a med-ical appointment, but Dun Gifford asked him to testify. He had traveled by airplane, unwill-ingly, only twice before. ("If God had wanted us to fly," he always said, "he would have given us wings.") But, in the hopes that his testimony might help the bill's cause, he agreed to attend. Accompanying him from the Vineyard was Sydna White of Vineyard Haven, presi-dent of the Concerned Citizens.

The nearly day-long hearing was held in the House Interior and Insular Affairs Committee Room with its gilded ceiling molds of eagles and acanthus leaves and a wall of faded paintings of the Old West. The subcommittee Henry and the other thirteen witnesses faced was seated behind an impressive dark wood desk and beneath an array of colorful flags.

Sydna White pleaded eloquently for the bill's enactment. She pointed out that off-island communities, as their beauty was destroyed by development, could expand outward to surrounding areas if necessary, "but we on the Island can't spread. The sea stops us. Please help us to preserve this unique and lovely part of America."

Henry, in his statement, remembered the Vineyard's "more than 300 years of history, family life, care and productive labor which have produced the Islands' distinctive culture and character. . . . Even if 99.44 percent of the present registered voters in our towns were to turn their backs on the bill and seek to sell off its land and character for immediate prof-it, they would have no right to do so," because of this heritage, he said. And he asked the subcommittee to consider not only voters' sentiments about the bill but those of the non-island voting summer people who were paying sixty percent of the taxes. Senator Kennedy made a final plea to the subcommittee for "these rare, magnificent islands." Even Senator Brooke—by this time mollified that he had not been consulted in advance about the bill (apparently a Kennedy aide's oversight)—endorsed it. But Carroll, Chilmark Selectman Hancock, and County Commissioner Shirley Frisch were among those on hand to speak out fiercely against it. And their will prevailed.

On September 22, a week before the close of Congress, the subcommittee rejected the Nantucket Sound Islands Trust Bill. The following year, a revised version was introduced to the House by Gerry Studds, state representative, and to the Senate by Kennedy and Brooke, but it died in committee. Kennedy did not try again. Nantucketers, with seasonal resident Gifford as the bill's architect, in the beginning were in favor of the bill. Then, as on the Vineyard, hotel owners and real estate developers campaigned against it; the Nantucket referendum voted it down. That, Henry always felt, was more than either Gifford or Kennedy could take.

"The Vineyard is going to Hell fast," Henry said after the failure of the Kennedy Bill. "But since I sold the *Gazette*, I have less feeling of responsibility than in the past. Nowadays, only the responsibility of the human race for the human race, which is bad enough."

Chapter 24

Soliciting for Conservation

The 1976 defeat of the Kennedy Bill was devastating for Henry Hough, as was the failure of his efforts to establish a historic district in his beloved Edgartown. Henry was nearly eighty years old. He was angry at the shortsightedness leading to both defeats and, briefly, he was as discouraged as he ever had been over the years.

But always, he would find a new and invigorating challenge to face. A few years earlier, he had written to author Jessamyn West about life and the world. Reading her works, Hough sensed they were kindred spirits. In his letter he had commented on his own "elusive optimism." It sometimes faded (as it did when a book or a story he had written was rejected), but he never lost all hope. He simply kept on trying. Had the Islands Trust Bill been enacted, the last years of his life might have been more serene but, scrapper that he was, he would have been restless.

As Henry looked back on the Vineyard's growth in the two previous decades, he realized that much good had come to the island, too. Zoning was widespread now, helping to protect townscapes and neighborhoods. The Vineyard Open Land Foundation had been established to preserve the natural beauty and rural character of the Vineyard by acquiring and protecting strategic parcels of land. The Felix Neck Wildlife Sanctuary had been founded in 1969. Henry had played a role in all of these.

Despite the failure of the Kennedy Bill, the resulting attention to the environmental dangers facing the island led to the enactment of the State Bill and the formation of the Martha's Vineyard Commission to oversee development projects.

Now in semi-retirement and recognized as the island's elder statesman for conservation, Hough wielded his personal touch to continue protecting Vineyard land and seascape. Years ago he had expanded and protected the wetland surrounding the original Sheriff's

Meadow tract by approaching his neighbors one by one to ask them to give contiguous land. In 1967, when a new Massachusetts law allowed neighborhood zoning if four or more residents of the area requested it, he had persuaded his Sheriff's Lane neighbors to institute it, warning them of the possible results without it (zoning along their lane would allow single-family residences there but no trailers). As time went on, he perfected this technique of encouraging and importuning the powerful and wealthy, and anyone else in a position to save Vineyard lands.

But ahead lay much bigger projects. In 1971, the 218-acre Mohu estate on the North Shore—woods, hills, and meadows Henry and George so often crossed long ago—was put on the market for $1,500,000. Once the property of Senator William M. Butler, the estate was formed by his purchase of one farm after another, Henry remembered from his boyhood. A Falmouth developer was now eager to subdivide it; Henry Hough was determined he wouldn't get it.

"To let that splendid piece of the Vineyard go forever to blacktop roads and chopped-up half-acre lots with pre-fab and rock-type dwellings, would be tragic," he exclaimed.

In the early 1960s, *Washington Post* publisher Katharine Graham had rented a house on Edgartown's Eel Pond, a quiet, out-of-the-way body of water near Sheriff's Meadow. She and her children had enjoyed the beach and the yacht club. She considered looking for property on the Vineyard, but with houses in Washington and Virginia, she never pursued it. Graham did tell her friend Scotty Reston, after he bought the *Gazette*, of her vague interest. Reston suggested she talk to Henry Hough and arranged for them to meet. Admirer of good newspapers as he was, Henry was delighted to make the acquaintance of the *Post*'s publisher, and he liked the idea of her as a sometime Vineyarder. He listened carefully to her requirements for property, among them privacy and a beach. When Hough learned of the fate awaiting Mohu, Graham was the potential purchaser who first came to mind, and so he wrote to her.

"He said this great place with umpteen rooms was for sale and that he feared development. Would I take a look at it?" she recalled. "I threw the letter away. By that time I was alone and two-hundred acres were involved.

"But then he sent me a picture of the land, and he talked to Libby MacFarlane, the owner, and she sent me pictures of the dunes and the beach. I liked what I saw, and I said to myself that surely Mrs. MacFarlane would sell me just ten acres or so, so I came up to look. But when she wouldn't sell me just a part of it, I placed a bid for everything. Henry was delighted. Then I got nervous, and withdrew the bid."

But Henry Hough was not ready to lose Mohu. To reacquaint himself with the terrain so he could describe it more temptingly, he began spending mornings and sometimes afternoons climbing its hills. He was determined to have Mohu pass into the hands of someone who would cherish it; if not Mrs. Graham, perhaps Fairleigh Dickinson Jr., the New Jersey university founder, Edgartown homeowner, and one-time potential *Gazette* owner. Henry

Even in his eighties, Henry worked indefatigably to preserve such sights as the Memorial Day lupines in bloom at Lambert's Cove in West Tisbury. *Photograph by E. Malcolm Phillips, courtesy of the* Vineyard Gazette

visited him at his Starbuck's Neck house overlooking Edgartown harbor to describe it; Dickinson said he would consider it.

Meanwhile, Mrs. MacFarlane, though she wished to preserve the property as one piece and realized that selling to the Falmouth developer would mean houses everywhere, was increasingly pressed financially. She talked with representatives of the Open Land Foundation to see if they could buy the land from her. Then she learned that Henry had met with Fairleigh Dickinson. On the strength of that meeting alone—and her hopes of what might result—she turned down the developer's offer of $50,000 for fifty acres. Her plan had been to sell him that much for development, as he wished, and sell the rest to a single buyer for $1 million. But the possibility that Dickinson might buy it all gave her the courage to send the developer away.

"How ruinous that would have been if he had gotten any of it," Henry later wrote to Dickinson. "The integrity of the property would have been utterly destroyed. But your interest encouraged her to hold on." And while MacFarlane was holding on, Hough asked

Kay Graham, back on the Vineyard, to look at Mohu again. Anyone with an interest in nature could hardly turn down a Henry Hough invitation to go on a woodland walk, particularly one along the North Shore he knew so well. He could identify virtually every tree and wildflower on his energetic, purposeful treks, and told stories of every boulder and pasture and hillock. He would recall those heavy-laden sailing schooners he had seen sailing off shore when he was a boy.

So as she and Henry walked, he told her his memories of Senator Butler and of the old farmsteads he bought to form his estate. They jumped brooks and examined old kettle holes, thrashed across thickets of huckleberry, dingleberry, and bayberry. They walked along the golden crescent shore and watched the seagulls purposefully diving. Kay Graham was treated to the best of Henry the naturalist.

Henry's North Tisbury neighbor Amyas Ames remembered that wonderful characteristic: "He never missed a thing on a walk. He was always so very deeply engrossed in natural things. He never passed a mushroom, or an orchid without stopping. He'd come across a spider and stop and talk about what kind of spider it was. He'd see it all and he loved it all."

Ultimately, Kay Graham could not withstand either the beauty of Mohu or Henry Hough's pleas to save it. But weeks went by while she considered and reconsidered; Henry was afraid he was not convincing enough. He continued to spend mornings touring the property with her. Then, at lunchtime, he would wearily drive to the *Gazette* office, wondering if he had shown her the most entrancing overlooks, berating himself for missing the prospect that might have compelled her to buy Mohu. Finally, however, in July 1972, Katharine Graham gave in to his incessant wooing and bought the estate for $1,460,000. An ecstatic Henry wrote to Dickinson to thank him for his instrumental role in the sale. "Here, at last," Henry wrote, "we have a wonderful property saved, and together with it, an important gain for the Vineyard, which so badly needs gains of this kind."

In 1967 he had seen the completion of another favorite conservation project, the acquisition of the Obed, Sherman, and Maria Roberts Daggett Sanctuary at Cedar Tree Neck, also on the North Shore, by the Sheriff's Meadow Foundation. Again, Henry had launched the project by donating something of his own—the land near Fish Hook he had inherited from his father. Next, he persuaded his brother to give part of his land for the sanctuary. And he had written to the heirs of their old friend Obed Daggett, who had taken them fishing in their youth, and urged them, for the sake of the Vineyard, to sell their inheritance at considerably below market value. After years of his insistent writing and calling, they agreed. Armed with that success, he turned again to Dickinson, this time for financial advice: how to raise the $165,000 the Daggett family wanted for their hundred acres. According to businessman Dickinson, about a third of the money was needed as a "starter." Then Dickinson offered it to him. To launch his requests for the rest, Hough wrote to U.S. Secretary of the Interior Stewart Udall asking his support.

From boyhood, Henry had cherished the beauty of the North Shore's Cedar Tree Neck.
Photograph by M.C. Wallo

"To get Cedar Tree Neck, the magnificent headland, with moors, ponds and hills, which is the Island's farthest projection into Vineyard Sound . . . and which has been in the Daggett family for a couple of hundred years, we here on Martha's Vineyard must carry on a campaign through the Vineyard Conservation Society and we would like a strong list of sponsoring names. Is this something you can endorse?" Henry asked. A number of important sponsors were already behind the project: former Atomic Energy Commission chairman David Lilienthal, *New York Times* editorial page editor John B. Oakes, editor and publisher Michael Straight, actress Katharine Cornell, MIT president Jerome B. Wiesner, *Ladies' Home Journal* editors Bruce and Beatrice Gould, and naturalist Richard Pough. Udall agreed to let his name be used.

Next, in article after article in the *Gazette* (using Betty's technique for raising money for the Red Stocking Fund or Miss Foote's animal shelter), and in personal letters, Henry sought more contributions. These solicitations, former Sheriff's Meadow board member Edith Potter remembered, always seemed to come out in midwinter. "I asked him about that once," she said, "and he told me that midwinter was the perfect time, in articles or in letters, to seek contributions for the Island from off-islanders." Midwinter, Henry felt, was just when the summer people longed to be on the Vineyard and were most inclined to be generous about island matters.

Once the initial Daggett land and its homestead were acquired, Henry began making the usual overtures to owners of contiguous land. Ultimately, the Cedar Tree Neck Sanctuary had grown to nearly two hundred acres and, with the addition of several other parcels, became the largest of all Sheriff's Meadow lands. Henry was pleased and he knew Betty would have been proud.

"Preserved as a natural area, that recourse of wood, ravine, glade and beach will never be to future generations what it was to George and me," Hough wrote then of his boyhood paradise. "Experience, like history, repeats itself in different patterns. . . . The sunshine glints at strange angles instead of from the majesty of high noon. . . . But no matter what change, there is a substance that remains . . . and that should be preserved for the future to live over again in its own way."

One autumn soon after the completion of the purchase, Hough neighbor Lilienthal went for a walk through the sanctuary. He crunched through the fallen golden leaves of its beech wood and followed the stubbly path to its knoll above Vineyard Sound. When he got home, he wrote a letter to Henry. "My first impulse, as I drew in the delight of that scene, was to thank the Lord for Henry Hough, for his comprehension, his patient impatience . . . and his love for the Island. I recalled what he had said once about how he knew he couldn't solve all the problems of this world, but he would settle for improving and protecting a small part of it. . . . If for no other reason than the joy of this morning's ramble, I am grateful to you."

Chapter 25

Repulsing Big Mac

It was likened by some to the fight between David and Goliath—the battle between little Martha's Vineyard and McDonald's of the Golden Arches. Yankee Henry Hough, however, saw in his fellow-islanders' standoff against the multimillion-dollar fast-food chain the independent spirit of the Boston Tea Party.

In 1978, the McDonald's Corporation proudly announced its plan to open its 5,110th restaurant on Martha's Vineyard. The announcement came just in time to spoil the enjoyment of fall for Henry Beetle Hough.

Since he went off-island rarely, Henry admitted that he had never eaten a Big Mac, but he didn't feel deprived. He had never favored conformity. If McDonald's put an eatery on the Vineyard, it would be a giant step in that direction. McDonald's in the 1970s was what the orange and blue Howard Johnson's of the highways had been in the 1940s and '50s. In those days, when he and Betty had gone off-island, they had seen Howard Johnson's restaurants aplenty and always feared one might find its way to the Vineyard.

From what Henry knew of them, if McDonald's wanted to be on the island, there would be no stopping them. The natural food store premises on the Beach Road in Vineyard Haven was the likely site. Hough remembered that before it sold health food, the shop was the Martha's Vineyard Cooperative Society, founded in 1941—an idealistic endeavor designed to sell foodstuffs for less than the commercial groceries and to support local farmers by buying their produce. Vineyarders could join the co-op as members and ordered from it in bulk. Peter Barry Chowka, one of McDonald's staunchest opponents, noted the irony of an off-island fast-food franchise usurping the lease held by a quality natural foods store in a building that, for two decades, had housed a co-op market.

The Tisbury Board of Health weighs a controversial proposal to open a McDonald's on the town's Beach Road. *Photograph by Hollis L. Engley, courtesy of the* Vineyard Gazette

Given McDonald's wealth, off-island popularity, and public relations expertise, Henry Hough doubted at first how effective an anti-McDonald's editorial campaign would be. But, even at eighty-two, Henry Hough was itching to wage another war.

When mail from opponents of the franchise began to pour into the *Gazette* office, he was delighted. If McDonald's came to the Vineyard, what next? letters asked. Would a Pizza Hut replace the Harbor View in Edgartown, a Wendy's appear at Menemsha across from the Home Port, a Burger King arise next to the Tabernacle in the Oak Bluffs Camp Ground?

It wasn't long before 1,500 signatures were collected on a petition against allowing the franchise on the Vineyard. Objections were numerous: for example, the proposed site, right on the edge of Vineyard Haven harbor, was inappropriate for an enterprise requiring large quantities of water. The Tisbury Board of Health already had instituted a moratorium on further building at the harbor's edge. There was talk of styrofoam cups and paper napkins and sandwich boxes strewn along the shore. But former New Bedford mayor Edward F. Harrington, who was seeking to buy the real estate for the franchise, steamed right ahead. When the No-Mac Committee declared that the Vineyard didn't need McDonald's because the island was a place of individuality and tradition, a special place, Harrington retorted, "Well, you won't be special long."

Undeterred by the brouhaha, McDonald's filed for a septic disposal works permit. A hearing on the application was scheduled with the town's board of health. The spokesman for the fast-food franchise explained to those concerned about golden arches on the island that the company had no intention of altering the looks of the co-op building, and would just add a discreet McDonald's sign. In the interests of customer parking convenience, however, and to avoid additional traffic congestion on the already busy Vineyard Haven–Oak Bluffs road, the company would move the building. The parking lot would be in front of the restaurant for better visibility getting in and out rather than "tucked in behind."

In response to the complaint that this off-island-based fast-food eatery would take business away from existing island-owned food establishments, and furthermore would not employ a significant number of islanders, the spokesman maintained that the company's franchises always contributed considerably to local economies, paying substantial real estate taxes and purchasing from local purveyors.

At the first board of health meeting on the matter, an overflow crowd of young and old, many sporting Expel Big Mac T-shirts, filled the little Tisbury Town Hall annex. The application was turned down on a technicality. A week later, at a second hearing, television cameras honed in on the two adversaries, McDonald's versus the Tisbury Board of Health. Board of health inspector Dr. Michael Jacobs re-emphasized that the board was simply being consistent in denying the septic system permit, since a moratorium on additional building along the harbor front was already in place. "We are not prepared to issue any permits that would increase the waste water in this area," Dr. Jacobs said.

Meanwhile, the off-island publicity (even *Variety* carried a piece about it) combined with Henry Hough's ability to persuade famous names to support environmental causes, resulted in several seasonal residents supporting the Down With McDonald's cause, including actress Mia Farrow, performers Beverly Sills, James Taylor, and Carly Simon, cartoonist Jules Feiffer, and novelists William Styron and Robert Crichton.

Henry Hough's peaceful autumn was disturbed as the fray began. But after that, in his inimitable way, he enjoyed the confrontation. "This is as good a fight as any, better than most," he wrote to off-island friends. "This is just the thing before Christmas and the New Year to fill in before the town meetings."

By the end of January, the corporate giant had retreated. The *New York Times* reported "Martha's Vineyard Repulses Big Mac" and Henry Hough added, "Yes, we did repel Big Mac, which proves, as someone said, that you can't lose them all. This was a good one to win!"

Chapter 26

A Second Marriage

In the years since Betty's death, the sale of the *Gazette* and events on the Vineyard kept Henry Hough well occupied. He thought he could not manage alone, but he did—albeit in a most bachelorlike living style. At first, he and Lochinvar, the last collie he and Betty had owned together, made do in the Pierce Lane house. (Betty had persuaded the town to change the name of their little road from the inappropriate "avenue" to "lane.") In 1971, eleven-year-old Lochie, grown increasingly feeble, had to be put down. Henry mourned him, but after two months, he knew he needed another dog to walk to the lighthouse mornings and to keep him company in the long silences of the night. *Gazette* reporter-photographer Edie Blake, who was becoming more and more important in Henry's social life, got him a parrot, the pets she enjoyed, but he did not like confining a bird in a cage. Henry loved dogs, and had always had one. Dogs were the best of company, of course, on all his walks. Edie Blake encouraged him to get a new collie, and promised that, should the dog outlive him, she would care for it. Happy with this arrangement, Henry made one of his rare trips to Cape Cod to look at a litter of collie pups. He selected one from among the newborns and a few weeks later brought back from the Cape an ingratiating gold and white ball of fur he named Graham. Graham was Edith Blake's maiden name, and there had been Grahams, too, in Betty's family tree. Henry dedicated one of his last books, *Soundings at Sea Level*, "To the Three Grahams in My Life."

Graham was soon quite at home, bounding along with Henry on his walks and returning to happily sneeze and gambol around the kitchen. He would patiently watch as his master sorted the mail on the flat-topped washing machine, but he was genuinely interested when he headed for the refrigerator. Henry would open its broken door gingerly; opening and closing the door involved a makeshift window weight tied to the handle and then looped around a heating pipe in the ceiling. In the refrigerator were tasty tidbits of interest to dogs.

Even though Henry was well into his eighties by then, he took on the challenge of the new puppy calmly. He told Edie he would have Graham housebroken and leash-trained within a day, and he did. His new dog was an unsquelchable companion. Mornings, just before breakfast, he joined his master collecting the data from the weather station in the back yard and filling the bird feeders. Then Graham would enjoy his kibble breakfast while Henry ate his shredded wheat and toast and—depending on the season—watched white-throated sparrows, cardinals, chickadees, and myrtle warblers enjoying theirs.

Twice a week, Lillian Kimball came in to clean. Henry agreed he was not much of a cleaner or dishwasher. He tended to let dishes accumulate in the sink and newspapers pile up. He readily admitted that he did not mind litter or clutter inside a house or an office; he and Betty, busy with their work and their causes, had always lived that way. The floor of his little upstairs study was always covered with paper—both new and used. But through the window behind his desk, he would look out and be pleased that the view of the old Ice Pond and Nantucket Sound was uncluttered.

At night, in the beginning, Henry and the puppy shared the same single bed in the bedroom on the northeast side of the house, but, as Graham grew, the bed became too small for both man and dog. Henry bought a three-quarter-size bed for both of them. But Graham was disdainful of it and returned to the old single bed, leaving Henry by himself.

The presence of the puppy helped relieve the melancholy that haunted Henry for some time after Betty's death. As Betty's analyst had told her, so Henry's told him that his depression was related to the way he had treated himself in life—his realization of everything he had failed to do simply for pleasure. It was at night that the depressions came and as soon as sunrise was near they lifted and he was quickly up and about his day of carefully planned work.

After Scotty and Sally Reston had bought the *Gazette,* workplace problems surfaced, a new experience for Henry. For years he had been accustomed to a friendly shop, the kind of place where Joe Allen would produce a little thank-you doggerel for Christmas bonuses:

> Employers most revered once more my thanks receive
> For this colossal bonus check that comes on Christmas Eve.
> It should have anyone admit that virtue always pays
> An adage that one seldom hears in these, the modern days
> And yet, and yet, I wonder now what virtues I possess
> I glance back briefly on my life to view an awful mess
> The things I did or did not do, producing grief and pain
> And yet I think, had I the chance, I'd do them all again.

In 1975, Richard and Mary Jo ("Jody") Reston took over the management of the *Gazette. Photograph by Alison Shaw, courtesy of the* Vineyard Gazette

And Joe might add at the end of the doggerel how grateful he was to have worked through the years in a "communal shop."

The only personnel problems at the *Gazette* in the Houghs' early days—and the employees never knew—were a result of the July money from advertising coming in late. The only way Henry and Betty could meet the payroll was to let their own bills go unpaid and to buy only essentials like gasoline and light bulbs in small quantities.

But the Restons were not the Houghs. They were viewed by some of the younger *Gazette* employees as well-to-do off-islanders who bought the paper as a plaything. Staff members had little patience with them and there was talk of forming a trade union so salaries—always low at the paper—could be raised. Edie Blake, by then at the *Gazette* full-time, was outspoken about the paper's mismanagement, and longtime employees feared she might be put in charge and some of them let go. Happily, in the end, the "unionization" came to nothing and Edie resigned. Henry's feelings, however, were hurt. The contretemps over Edie had prevented him from settling down to write the text for a book of island photographs by *Life* photographer Alfred Eisenstaedt.

In his letter of apology to Eisenstaedt, Henry's rising affection for Edie became clear, as he complained that he was so absorbed in Edie's "contemptible" treatment he could not concentrate. The Restons were too far away to understand what was involved, he wrote, and praised Edie: "Since she is a good sport as well as a lady she stepped aside with as much dignity and grace as I have ever seen in a human being."

Gradually, after that, the *Gazette* workplace returned to normal. Finally, in the fall of 1975, came Henry's longed-for relief from *Gazette* cares. From the time the Restons bought the paper, three interim managing editors had handled the day-to-day news gathering and directed the staff, much as Betty had done. However, all were young and depended on Henry for guidance. At last Richard Reston, the eldest of the sons, and his wife Mary Jo decided it was time to try country journalism. Mary Jo, called Jody, took over the paper's business management. She had been a schoolteacher and in Washington worked for Blue Cross–Blue Shield, in charge of insurance for all government employees. Dick Reston became the *Gazette* editor. For a while, Douglas Cabral, one of the interim managing editors, stayed on. Later he became editor of the *Martha's Vineyard Times,* a paper begun by Vineyard business interests. Henry had been concerned about such competition ever since the Kennedy Bill conflict, when an anti-establishment paper called the *Grapevine* was started. After all, when he and Betty acquired the *Gazette,* they bought out the other island papers. Reston, accustomed to the cutthroat world of Big City journalism, was matter of fact about any other rival paper.

By the time Dick Reston arrived, his father had changed the *Gazette's* production to the offset printing method. For Henry Hough, Linotype operator and line-casting machine inventor, the decision was heartbreaking. Intellectually, he knew Reston was right and that the paper must move with the times, but he remembered how he and Betty had scrimped and borrowed to buy the press and the Linotype machine, now to be scrapped to make way for offset. The press was taken apart with a blow torch, the Linotype removed with a crane. "There it was, dangling in the air," Henry recalled of that day. "Graham and I walked home, and I wrote that I felt like a fadeout in an old movie, nostalgic and a little melancholic." After that, he knew he was glad to be out of the day-to-day operation of the paper. "I am still a hot metal man myself," he commented, "having operated and suffered with a Linotype for so many years. I couldn't get used to this cutting up of little scraps of paper and sticking them on a dummy sheet."

He did like the idea of switching from typewriters to computers which sent copy directly from the newsroom to the back shop, however—very much like the link he had envisioned as a young man when he had developed his own Linotype. Altogether, though he didn't want to be completely retired from the paper, he was pleased to have someone else responsible for it. Time was running out. He would keep on writing *Gazette* editorials, but he was eager to spend most of his time writing books.

Meanwhile, vibrant socialite Blake, thirty years younger, was inviting him to Christmas dinners and to afternoon teas (until one day he asked if she would substitute whiskey for the tea). That broke the ice and next he hesitantly asked her to a restaurant for dinner.

Edie Blake's great grandparents came to Edgartown summers in the 1890s from Bernardsville, New Jersey. From the age of ten, Edie had spent her summers sailing and swimming and playing tennis in Edgartown. (Henry discovered she was the grandniece of socialite Longe de Saulle, whose murder by his beautiful Chilean ex-wife, Blanquita, was one of the more exciting stories Henry had covered as a student at Columbia.)

Edie married Robert Howard Blake Jr. in 1945 when he was in the Navy. His mother's brother had started the Campbell Soup Company and his father was the Cunard Line's top executive in the United States. She and Blake had moved to Tuxedo Park, New York, and had a daughter. Summers, they came to the Vineyard; after their 1954 divorce, she and her daughter continued to come. During these years, as a crack tennis player, she began covering tennis for the *Gazette*. In the summer of 1965 Edie was hired full-time at the paper, and she decided to stay on through the winter, too.

For the next six years, she moved from house to house in Edgartown—staying in the boathouse at her mother's elegant North Water Street house when it was available and otherwise renting or caretaking the houses of friends; her mother held tightly onto the family money. By 1971, Hough was feeling increasingly protective of her. He wanted her to have a home of her own so he gave her land on Sheriff's Meadow Lane. He and Betty had planned to add it to their previous gifts of land to Sheriff's Meadow, but never got to it. Now, Henry felt, Edie needed it.

Here she built a cheery two-bedroom house she shared with her yellow-fronted

Gazette reporter-photographer Edith G. Blake, the second Mrs. Hough, strolls with her husband on a summery Edgartown street. *Copyright Alfred Eisenstaedt*

Amazon parrot, Madeleine. Henry was a little surprised at how much he liked having Edie nearby. At first, their social life together was largely taking walks with his dogs, for they both loved animals. But Henry found that he was taking more and more delight in her irrepressible blond bubbliness. She would be invited to a cocktail party and would ask him to be her escort. He would be invited out and would suggest that she accompany him. Their social worlds were vastly different, however. She belonged to the Edgartown Yacht Club and its tennis club; her friends tended to be, as she was, the socialites of Edgartown.

Henry's friends were still the intellectuals who lived all over the Vineyard. After Betty's death, of course, old friends continued to include Henry in their social circle, such as Yvette Eastman, widow of essayist Max Eastman and Gay Head seasonal resident, and *New York Times* movie critic Bosley Crowther. Henry particularly treasured from this period a letter from playwright Lillian Hellman, after he had attained a modicum of success saving some piece of the Vineyard. She told him that he had long been one of her heroes "and I have not had many." Once when he was at odds with Martha's Vineyard National Bank president Luce, the playwright had offered to close her account in support of Henry. Henry also enjoyed the company of conservationist John B. Oakes, editor of the *New York Times* editorial page, and of American Civil Liberties founder Roger Baldwin; Henry had worked closely with him to preserve in public partnership some of the rural areas of the island. Otis L. Guernsey Jr. of Edgartown and Vermont, a New York *Herald Tribune* drama critic and anthologist of annual editions of the year's best plays, was a close friend, as were conservation writer Nan Simon and Hiram Haydn, one of the founders of Atheneum, the publisher of Henry's second New Bedford novel, *Lament for a City*. Artist Thomas Hart Benton was a close friend of Henry's father (he painted a portrait of him acquired by the Boston Museum of Fine Arts), and remained Henry's friend after George Sr.'s death.

Although Henry continued to drive until nearly the time of his death, as he grew older Edie Blake often drove him to this party or that. He enjoyed her ebullient, spontaneous personality, so different from Betty's. He was torn between the realization that Edie was much too young to be his constant companion, and yearning for her. Under any circumstances, he wanted to make sure she was financially secure. When she wanted to write a book about the filming of *Jaws* on the Vineyard, he encouraged her, edited for her, and helped with the publicity.

The first edition of *On Location on Martha's Vineyard: the Making of the Movie "Jaws"* was printed by Cape Cod's Lower Cape Publishing Company, but Henry felt it should be getting more attention than a local publisher could provide. He sent copies of the book to various publications he knew, among them *Editor and Publisher*. There, movie critic and West Tisbury seasonal resident Gene Shalit read about the book and mentioned it on the *Today Show*. Soon Ballantine Books was interested in reprinting it. Henry was delighted for

Octogenarian Henry Hough at home. *Photograph by Alison Shaw, courtesy of the*
Vineyard Gazette

Edie, and with himself, that he could help her. In 1969, he offered to pay her a $5,000 annual salary to take pictures to support such conservation causes as the Massachusetts Audubon Society and The Nature Conservancy. Gleefully, he wrote to Fairleigh Dickinson, "I am able to finance this myself, and it will be a rewarding novelty."

But he was also urging Edie, in a fatherly way, "to pursue all the friendships she possibly could." Whenever she did, however, and talked of someone new she met on the tennis court or at a cocktail party or the Edgartown Yacht Club, he would be jealous and concerned that she might be taken advantage of. When a man who had separated from his wife began squiring her, Henry wrote to him like an outraged Victorian father, scolding him roundly for risking Edie's reputation since he was still, technically, a married man.

Then, finally, Henry asked her if she would marry him.

The first time he asked, she was uncertain. She liked her freedom and knew Henry liked his, too. She knew enough about the disorder in his house across the lane from hers—the pile of old beach chairs against the back gate to keep it closed so Graham wouldn't get out, the makeshift refrigerator door latch—to know she could never live that way. She turned him down. But Henry persisted, and on a winter night in 1979 when the sky sparkled with stars and the big clock on the Old Whaling Church tower was in clear view over Edgartown, Henry proposed for what he said would be a final time, and Edie Blake accepted. However, the way each lived would not change, she said.

So, on a cold, rainy December 13 (thirteen, Edie said, was her lucky number), they took the ferry to Woods Hole and were married before the Franklin stove in the seventeenth-century Falmouth home of Henry's nephew John, and his wife Mally. Edie felt it was important to be married under a family roof and the closest one was John (Jack) Hough's. Jack had succeeded Henry's brother, George, as editor and publisher of the *Falmouth Enterprise*. Jack's son, John, was a beginning novelist. Seeing something of himself in his grandnephew, Henry gave him the Rogers house he and Betty had so loved at Indian Hill.

Former Edgartown Yacht Club Commodore Jared Bliss and his wife—another Edie—gave the bride away and had a luncheon before the wedding at the nearby Coonamesset Inn. The Rev. John R. Golding of Edgartown performed the ceremony.

At the inn luncheon, John Golding asked Henry if he had a ring for his bride; he produced a tiny platinum ring that was much too small for Edie's finger. It had been Betty's wedding ring, he said, and—for continuity's sake—he wanted Edie to have it. But since it wouldn't fit, a diamond and emerald ring he had given her was substituted.

A few days later, Hough wrote to Scotty Reston: "Our marriage will make no difference at all in our lives. She will live in her immaculate and perfectly appointed house and I will live in my relaxed and determinedly comfortable one. What we are doing is simply to protect a friendship which has become valuable and necessary these past years. Bob Nevin said once that loneliness is, in itself, an illness.

time, Henry and thirteen other Edgartonians also appealed; in their view the restriction imposed was not enough.

A representative of the Massachusetts Department of Environmental Quality Engineering investigated the matter. He looked briefly at the site, said he didn't think the problem concerned his department, and told the town commission that he was overriding its restriction.

In spite of his dislike of leaving the island, a furious Hough flew to Boston to reiterate at a Department of Environmental Quality hearing that the land in question was, indeed, a wetland. By that time, 259 Edgartown residents had written to the Army Corps of Engineers—mandated to protect wetlands—and decried Carroll's proposed construction. New houses there, they charged, would destroy the view, prized for generations, of the historic harbor mouth where Edgartown whaleships had once sailed. But the complaints went unheeded. Eight years after the battle began, a self-satisfied Carroll received approval for his houses and tennis court from the Army Engineers, the DEQE, and the Edgartown building inspector. Immediately, fill was dumped near the lagoon where Henry fed the marsh birds and the ducks. However, Henry and his fellow environmentalists were not ready to capitulate; their lawyer found a local zoning law he believed protected Edgartown's shoreland from development. The federal district court then found that the Army Corps of Engineers had not considered all of the ecological and historic preservation issues surrounding the property.

But Carroll—Kennedy Bill opponent, butcher's son, real estate broker, hotel and restaurant owner, Edgartown selectman and assessor—was determined to win this fight against Henry, too. Never one to mince words, he called Henry Hough "a son of a bitch elitist" and maintained that his opposition to the proposed houses was because he didn't want man-of-the-people Carroll living on chic North Water Street. He dismissed the pond as "a little mud puddle" and maintained that as far as ruining the view of the lighthouse was concerned, it would be "ridiculous" of him to destroy something that was a benefit to his own hotel. He filed a $750,000 countersuit to the one the environmentalists had started, vowing a fight to the death against the wealthy trying to preserve the status quo. What was going on had nothing to do with the environment at all, he insisted; it all had to do with "class."

As it turned out, one of Edgartown's "classiest" seasonal visitors, Fairleigh (Dick) Dickinson, who owned a house at Starbuck's Neck, resolved the controversy to the satisfaction of all. In 1975, for three-quarters of a million dollars, he had bought five important Edgartown properties and their grounds, all part of the estate of one of the town's prosperous fishing boat captains. His intention was to preserve the character of the town. As a friend of both Bob Carroll and Henry Hough—and as one who had often assisted Henry's conservation efforts—Dickinson now offered to give Carroll those properties plus more than $500,000 in exchange for the Harbor View wetland.

By then even Carroll was weary of fighting. The deal was a good one, and he agreed to it. Dickinson gave the Starbuck's Neck land to the town along with $10,000 to remove the fill already deposited and to return everything to its original wild state; Edgartown would keep the wetland in conservation. It was the third time Dickinson, in one way or another, had helped Henry save a piece of the Vineyard: his interest in Mohu had prevented its sale to a developer, and his advice on fundraising had meant the Sheriff's Meadow Foundation could acquire Cedar Tree Neck.

Harbor View Hotel owner Robert J. Carroll fought a fierce conservation battle with Henry in the last years of the editor's life. *Photograph by Alison Shaw, courtesy of the Vineyard Gazette*

That bitter Harbor View wetland fight, its happy resolution notwithstanding, took its toll on Henry Hough, eighty-seven by the time it was over. The early 1980s, altogether, were not the best of times for him. Though he was pleased that *Soundings at Sea Level* had come out, the book was only lukewarmly received, except for accolades from Scotty Reston in the *Gazette*. In 1981, Joe Allen, the Wheelhouse Loafer, the *Gazette's* tireless representative-at-large and the last of the old gang, had died at eighty-nine. He and Henry had worked together for more than half a century. They had frequently been at odds, for Allen was an independent Yankee opposed to zoning, town planning, and the Kennedy Bill. Allen liked the open Vineyard landscape of his childhood and had no use for Henry and Betty's conniption fits—as he considered them—whenever island trees were cut.

But no member of the paper's staff was so beloved by its readers. Gay Headers never forgot Allen's tribute to Wampanoag Captain Joseph G. Belain in his *Gazette* obituary. Noticing that a pigeon had alighted on his bier in the cemetery, Allen remarked on its significance—Belain had saved the carrier pigeon from extinction. He was at home in virtually every island wheelhouse, where he gathered the news for his weekly waterfront column. At his seventieth birthday party, his writer son, Everett Allen, remarked: "There is no rabbit, no small duck, no child trying to make a bow and arrow out of a lath and an umbrella rib, no fisherman from Fayal, no little old lady in a nice apron who makes gingerbread, who will say a word against him. . . . He is a kind of unlikely combination of St. George and the dragon, offering something for everybody, including fire-breathing and a strong right arm."

As Henry sorrowfully wrote Joe's obituary, memories of their long years together all came back. He remembered the gleeful way Allen had teased Betty and made her alternately fuss at him and laugh. He recalled his wide range of mind, philosophy, and wit, his versatility in reporting, writing, and observing, and his marvelous sense of humor. He remembered their disagreements, too, but he realized how much the *Gazette* was beholden to Joe. He "was one of the most valued and cherished and admired" of his *Gazette* companions, Henry wrote. Now only one was left of that early Gazette foursome of Henry and Betty, Bill Roberts and Joe—Henry himself.

In the 1980s problems at the *Gazette* office arose again, deeply concerning its editor emeritus. Although Dick and Jody Reston had forcefully and eagerly taken over the paper, Vineyard isolation in winter was difficult, especially for Dick, accustomed to the bustle of Moscow, London, and Washington. The stress imposed by island life had been described a decade earlier by Vineyard psychiatrist Milton Mazer in *People and Predicaments*. The book noted the high incidence of alcoholism resulting from the Vineyard's limited activities in the off season. Dick Reston, for a time, became one of its victims. An uneasy Henry began to question the wisdom of his sale of the paper. Was a safe future for the *Gazette* really assured?

Joe Allen offered something for everybody, "including fire-breathing and a strong right arm," his son, writer Everett Allen, remarked on the Wheelhouse Loafer's seventieth birthday. *Photograph by Gretchen Van Tassel, courtesy of the* Vineyard Gazette

But Henry could put his worries aside when he went out with Edie. He also began work on a new book, based on a series of lectures he had delivered at the Nathan Mayhew Seminars, an adult education school established by former Sarah Lawrence and Harvard professor Thomas R. Goethals, longtime Vineyard seasonal resident and grandson of the builder of the Panama Canal, General George Goethals. Edie thought the lectures might make a book and approached Vineyard publisher Katharine Tweed. Henry called the book *Far Out the Coils*. The phrase, taken from Walt Whitman, and referring to a New England fisherman tossing line out to sea, was the one Hough had wanted as the title for his 1958 seafaring novel *The New England Story*, but it had not appealed to the editor. This time, for a book about the wide-ranging oceanic heritage of the island, it did.

Henry Hough, however, was never to see a finished copy of it. In the summer of 1985, Edie had noticed a change in color of a quarter-sized birthmark on his right forearm. Henry had Bob Nevin look at it and was told not to worry. But by Christmas a lump had grown under his right arm and Edie made an appointment to have it removed at Falmouth Hospital. At a follow-up appointment at the end of January, Edie was told that the birthmark had developed into a melanoma and that the cancer had spread, though it probably would move relatively slowly. Henry might well live until the new year, but there was no way of stopping the cancer's advance. Edie's legs went weak at the news. They had been married only six years. And she had been looking forward to a month-long visit to Greece.

Exactly the opposite of her husband, Edith G. Blake Hough could never travel enough. Until her marriage to Henry, she lacked the money to travel, but Henry's generosity sent her, twice, to visit the English island of Jersey to see the animals of naturalist-writer Gerald Durrell. She traveled to Morocco and Spain, and visited the places Henry, so long before, had seen in South Africa. She photographed nature, art, and archaeology on her trips and then relived them by showing Henry the pictures she had taken. Looking at them, and absorbing Edie's enthusiasm, was enough traveling for him. Greece had been on her list of destinations for a long time. She asked the doctor if she dared go. He urged her to continue as she had planned rather than make up a transparent excuse for not going—Henry had not been told that his life was nearing its end.

On one of Edie's off-island trips that year, she and a young *Gazette* reporter, Rick Fleury, had struck up a conversation. Fleury had told her how much he was enjoying working at the *Gazette*, but he added that he wished Mr. Hough was in the office more often. Henry Hough, Fleury said, was one of his heroes. When Rick came by for a drink, as Edie had suggested, Henry liked talking with him. Rick was a sensitive twenty-three-year-old from Bellingham, Massachusetts, who had been a journalism major at the University of Colorado. He became acquainted with the Vineyard in the summer of 1981, working at a windsurfing shop in Edgartown. When he went back to Colorado the following fall and told one of his teachers where he had been, she asked if he had met Henry Hough.

Fleury barely knew who Hough was, so the teacher gave him *Country Editor* to read. As it had inspired so many young journalists for decades, the book inspired Rick Fleury. He decided to write his final journalism paper about the *Gazette*. He requested copies of the paper, and studied its writing style, layout, and advertising. Both Rick and his teachers were pleased with the result, and he sent copies of his piece to both Henry Hough and Scotty Reston along with a job application. Both men wrote and thanked him, but no job offer was forthcoming. A year later, however, after Fleury was an account executive with a public relations firm in New York City, Dick Reston offered him a job and he had taken it.

That first drink with Edie and Henry led to others. Among Fleury's *Gazette* beats was Gay Head, whose residents of Native American descent were trying to gain recognition as a tribe, and Edgartown, where plan after plan for further development were proposed. Accustomed to being on top of the news, Henry liked knowing what was going on, but he did not want to intrude at the *Gazette* now that the Restons were fully in charge. (Once Dick had conquered his alcohol problem, Henry did not seem to be needed, and he largely stayed away.) So he enjoyed Rick's Thursday evening visits when the young man could fill him in about the news in Friday's paper.

As soon as Edie learned about Henry's illness, she called Rick with the news, asking him if he could stay with Henry while she was gone. Fleury said he would be happy to help out. For the next month, he occupied the bedroom Henry always called Graham's room—the one the dog had refused to vacate even after he had been supplied with his own bed. When Rick came home from the *Gazette* evenings, the cub reporter and the editor emeritus would have their Johnny Walker Scotch together in the living room and Rick would prepare a good, wholesome dinner—far better than the pancake and bread soup meals of Betty's day, and far cosier than Henry and Edie's usual restaurant dinners. Rick always set the dining room table and lit candles. Occasionally guests were invited too.

For the first week or so, Henry seemed in as good shape as ever. Suddenly, however, he began to have severe pain in his legs. He continued to write his editorials, but he lacked the strength to walk to the *Gazette* with them. He had to sit his way up and down the stairs to his study and bedroom. Rick would take his editorials to the paper or reporter Mark Lovewell would pick them up from "the hollow tree," what Henry chose to call the washing machine just inside the kitchen door.

When Edie returned, she made a little downstairs study into a bedroom for Henry. Throughout the winter, he kept on writing, receiving visitors, and meeting with Kay Tweed about *Far Out the Coils*. When spring came, he welcomed the return of the robins to the backyard feeders and Rick took him out to the garden to see the snowdrops and the yellow and purple crocuses arrive. Graham had died and a shy new collie, Killiekrankie, kept him company. His friends and relatives came for visits under the elms that he and Betty had planted and nurtured. Either Rick or Edie took Killie for her walks around the pond and when they returned, Henry was sure to ask, "Were there any buds yet on the trees?"

One sunny April day Rick proposed that he wheel Henry around the pond in his wheel-chair so he could see it for himself. Henry declined. He had never liked being waited on. But a few weeks later he rethought his decision, and told Rick he was taking him up on his offer. Rick put Henry in a warm jacket and a favorite bright red cap and off they went. The ground was muddy and wet, and once or twice the wheels of the chair got stuck. Killie grew impatient and barked. But the threesome—old man, young man, and collie dog—made it as far as the dam between the pond and John Butler's mudhole. En route, Henry kept pulling down the budding tree branches they passed so he could smell them. When they reached the dam, they stopped to admire the sunset and to watch the moon appear in the darkening sky. While they watched, the Whaling Church bell rang through the trees between Pierce and Sheriff's lanes.

Soon after Rick had moved into the Pierce Lane house to keep Henry company, he and Henry had talked about Thoreau. Henry gave him a copy of the *Annotated Thoreau* and they often discussed it. After that last trip around Sheriff's Meadow Pond, Rick always referred to it as Henry Hough's Walden.

The Henry Hough Memorial Bench is just above Sheriff's Meadow Pond.
Photograph by Mark Alan Lovewell

Novelist John T. Hough Jr. was among the eulogists at his great-uncle Henry's funeral. *Courtesy of the Vineyard Gazette*

Henry Hough never again encircled his beloved pond. By the last days of May, he needed round-the-clock nurses. Getting outdoors was too much for him, and he spent most of his time in the living room, reading. Rick and his nurses saw to it, however, that the flowers from his garden came inside in bouquets. By then, he knew he was dying, and he was telling Rick matter-of-factly that of course he wasn't going to live to be 150. "The cells can only divide 50 or 60 times," he said. But then his spirits would rally and he would say "I've got to stop this and get back to writing."

At other times, he was short-tempered. Though he almost never had sworn before, except for an occasional half-hearted "Damn," now he snapped that Bob Carroll, and others who had opposed his lifelong efforts on behalf of the island, were "bastards" or "sons of bitches."

But on days when he was feeling better—but not well enough to be reading on his own—Rick would sit beside him, hold his hand, and read to him from *Walden*. At a passage he particularly liked, Henry would squeeze Rick's hand and Rick would reread it.

Henry Beetle Hough died on Thursday, June 7, 1985—in time to have his obituary appear in Friday's *Gazette*. The courageous Country Editor of Martha's Vineyard, the admirer and protector of its woods and its fields and its shores, was gone. The Vineyard would never again be so gallantly guarded.

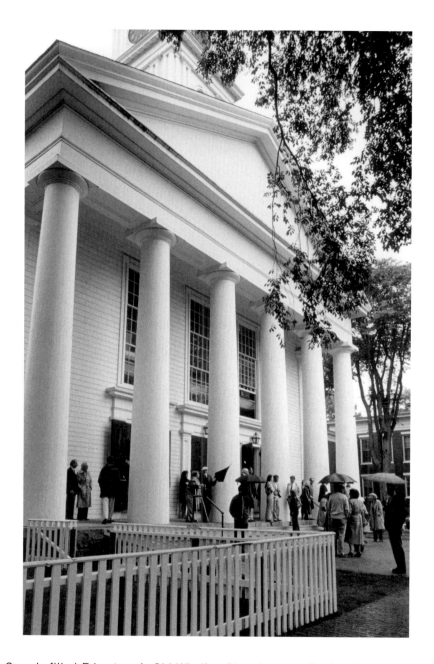

Crowds filled Edgartown's Old Whaling Church to overflowing for the 1985
funeral service for the *Vineyard Gazette*'s longtime editor and publisher.
Photograph by Alison Shaw, courtesy of the Vineyard Gazette

Henry and Graham enjoy the Fish Hook beach in the 1970s.
Photograph by Yvette Eastman

The Legacy of Henry Beetle Hough

Despite Mark Antony's assertion that the good that men do "is oft interred with their bones," the seed that Henry Beetle Hough planted has bloomed into a full-blown conservation movement that continues to grow and spread. Take Sheriff's Meadow Foundation: from its humble beginning protecting ten acres around the old ice pond forty-seven years ago, the Foundation has grown to become the largest private landowner on Martha's Vineyard, owning more than two thousand acres worth hundreds of millions of dollars. The foundation employs six year-round professional staff, dedicated to acquiring additional conservation land, as well as caring for the land already conserved.

In addition to Sheriff's Meadow Foundation, there are five other private nonprofit land conservation groups active on the island, as well as the publicly funded Martha's Vineyard Land Bank Commission. The Vineyard Conservation Society, Vineyard Open Land Foundation, The Trustees of Reservations, The Nature Conservancy, the Land Bank, the Commonwealth of Massachusetts, and the six island towns have permanently protected almost 20,000 acres, roughly one-third of the island, as public and private conservation land.

Despite these successes, many of us still see trouble in paradise. Although Vineyarders like to think of themselves as separate from "America," the truth is that Nantucket Sound is a narrow moat, and there is no drawbridge to raise. Sooner or later the issues facing the wider world find their way to Martha's Vineyard. In fact, because the Vineyard is a finite island, some problems are more acute here than on the mainland and the island has continued to change dramatically in the twenty years since Henry Hough's death.

Despite these changes, Hough's legacy is still very much in evidence. You still cannot buy a Big Mac or, for that matter, any other fast-food hamburger on the Vineyard. In fact, outside of two Stop and Shop supermarkets, there are no large chain stores on the island. Many of our roads still retain their rural character, with leafy green canopies arching overhead and open meadows and woodlands behind the ancient stone walls lining the roadsides. The controversy that exploded a few years ago when the highway department proposed cutting the stately old trees impinging on Music Street in West Tisbury was a battle that the Houghs would have clearly joined. One can easily imagine Henry's impassioned editorials against the proposed cutting.

The Martha's Vineyard Commission, created as part of a compromise that followed the failure of the Kennedy Bill, has repeatedly used its broad powers to turn back the most egregious development proposals of the past thirty years. We missed Hough's strong voice during the contentious commission hearings and public debate over the three new golf courses proposed for Martha's Vineyard. The controversy lasted nearly six years before finally ending in 2004, with the Land Bank purchasing 190 acres of the last of the proposed golf courses at a cost of $18.63 million.

Less widely recognized were the Houghs' efforts to prevent spraying of DDT and other pesticides. Because aerial spraying was limited to one occurrence, the Vineyard still has an abundance and variety of moths unequaled in all of New England. Perhaps one day these holdouts will repopulate the mainland just as the terns and shorebirds spread from their refugia on the offshore islands at the beginning of the twentieth century.

In his eulogy, John Hersey declared that nobody loved the Vineyard more than Henry Beetle Hough, nor feared more deeply for its future. There is no doubt that Henry Hough was profoundly disturbed by the changes he observed as he entered his final years, just as some of the changes of the last twenty years would have distressed him greatly. But I believe he would be heartened to know that he could still walk one of his beloved collies around the ice pond at Sheriff's Meadow, savor the view of Vineyard Sound from the bluff at Cedar Tree Neck, or walk the trails at Wascosim's Rock, Menemsha Hills, or one of the many other new conservation areas established in the past twenty years.

Henry did not win every battle, and we have certainly lost our share since his passing. Nonetheless, the Vineyard is still one of the most beautiful and biologically rich spots on the East Coast, and we remain grateful to Henry for his foresight and pioneering conservation efforts. Whether one views the Vineyard glass as half empty or half full, without the legacy bequeathed to us by Henry Beetle Hough the Vineyard would be a very different island today, and much less inviting.

Richard W. Johnson
Executive Director, Sheriff's Meadow Foundation

Acknowledgments

I am grateful to many for their aid in the preparation of this book: for encouragement, support, research, the checking of details, photographs, and editing and production.

For illustrations and photographs, I am grateful to Edith G. Blake, Bobbi Baker Burrows, the late Donald Carrick, Norma Costaine, Betsy Corsiglia, Nan Doty, Yvette Eastman, Hollis L. Engley, Ron Hall, George A. Hough 3rd, Lulu Kaye, Carol Lazar, Anne Lemenager, Mark Lennihan, Mark Alan Lovewell, Barbara, Chris, and Polly Murphy, Alison Shaw, Peter Simon, Thomas Thatcher, Gretchen Van Tassel, M.C. Wallo, the Tisbury Printer, and the *Vineyard Gazette*.

For information and for verifying details I would like to thank Phyllis J. Allen, James and John Alley, Leslie J. Baynes, Walter Bettencourt, Edith G. Blake, William H. Brine, the late Florence Scott Brown, Jean Bryant, Peter D. Bunzel, Doug Cabral, Tom Chase of The Nature Conservancy, Ruth Twichell Cochrane, Gus Ben David, Rick Fleury, Thomas L. Flynn Jr., the late Katharine Graham, Thomas Hale, Stan Hart, Garry Hough, George A. Hough 3d, John T. Hough, Robert H. Hughes, Richard W. Johnson of the Sheriff's Meadow Foundation, Cynthia Meisner, Robert Morgan, the late Robert Nevin, Brendan O'Neill of the Vineyard Conservation Society, Virginia Poole, Thomas B. Reston, Jon Sawyer, Robert S. Sanborn, Rose Burgunder Styron, Peter E. Strock, the Uniontown (Pennsylvania) Public Library, the University of Illinois Library, Dan A. Waters, Robert Woodruff, and the late Howard W. Young.

And support came from Edith G. Blake, Dorothy Brickman, Marylin Chou, Bridget Cooke, Carlyle Cronig, Jane K. Dean, Margaret Freydberg, Robert and Anne Ganz, Thomas R. Goethals, Fay Greene, Thomas Hale, Charlotte Hall, John R. Helm, Olga Hirshhorn, Margaret W. Hiser, Eugene Kalkin, Eleanor H. Ketcham, Richard Knabel, Barnett and Dolores Laschever, Sal Laterra, Sally Linden, Leo and Helen Milonas, Avrum and Dora Morrow, Margery Oakes, Don Page, Eleanor D. Pearlson, Mary Jane Pease, Robert and Edith Potter, Judith Randal, Richard and Mary Jo Reston, Jane Cole Scott, Donald and Constance Shanor, Lionel Spiro, Arthur O. Sulzberger Jr., Frances Tenenbaum, Katharine Tweed, the *Vineyard Gazette*, Elsie Walker, Ellen Weiss, Helen Young, Nancy Young, and from Keith Gorman, Warren H. Hollinshead, Betsey Mayhew, Peter Van Tassel, Art Railton, Matthew Stackpole, and Susan Wilson of the Martha's Vineyard Historical Society.

Thanks are also due to Kevin O'Connor and Henry Rowen of the Rare Book and Manuscript Library at Columbia University for help in consulting it; to Eulalie Regan of the *Vineyard Gazette* library for her endless patient research; to Clarence A. Barnes 3d, Nelson Bryant, Barbara Day, Richard Elfenbein, Kendra Frakes, George L. Gibson, Sheila Lennon, the late John E. Méras and the late Stanley Burnshaw, David McCullough, Wesley Mott, John C. Quinn, Bernard Sloan, Timothy Foote, Richard J. Walton, Henny Wenkart,

Robert Whitcomb, and Christina Ward for encouraging this work; and to Alex Goethals, Peter E. Méras, and Thomas and Katherine Vogl for technical help.

And I am, of course, especially appreciative of Images from the Past: Sarah Novak for her thoughtful and painstaking editing, Ron Toelke and Barbara Kempler-Toelke for their creative design, Helen Passey for indexing, and Tordis Ilg Isselhardt for the enthusiasm and insights without which there would have been no book; and to Christina Tree and William A. Davis for introducing me to Images from the Past.

Books by Henry Beetle Hough

Martha's Vineyard, Summer Resort. The Tuttle Publishing Company, 1936.

Country Editor. Blue Ribbon Books, 1940.

That Lofty Sky. The Book League of America, 1941.

At Christmas All Bells Say the Same. Doubleday, Doran & Company, 1942.

All Things Are Yours. Doubleday, Doran & Company, 1942.

Roosters Crow in Town. D. Appleton-Century Company, 1945.

Wamsutta of New Bedford. Wamsutta Mills, New Bedford, Massachusetts, 1946.

Long Anchorage. D. Appleton-Century Company, 1947.

Once More the Thunderer. Ives Washburn, Inc., 1950.

Singing in the Morning. Simon & Schuster, 1951.

An Alcoholic to His Sons (as told to Henry Beetle Hough). Simon & Schuster, 1954.

Thoreau of Walden. Simon & Schuster, 1956.

The New England Story. Random House, 1958.

Great Days of Whaling. Houghton Mifflin, 1958.

Melville in the South Pacific. Houghton Mifflin, 1960.

Lament for a City. Atheneum, 1960.

The Port. Atheneum, 1963.

Whaling Wives (with Emma Mayhew Whiting). Dukes County Historical Society, 1965.

Vineyard Gazette Reader (editor). Harcourt, Brace & World, 1967.

The Road. Harcourt, Brace & World, 1970.

Tuesday Will Be Different. Dial Press, 1971.

Mostly on Martha's Vineyard. Harcourt Brace Jovanovich, 1975.

Martha's Vineyard (with Alfred Eisenstaedt). Viking Press, 1975.

To the Harbor Light. Houghton Mifflin, 1976.

Soundings at Sea Level. Houghton Mifflin, 1980.

Remembrance and Light (with Alison Shaw). The Harvard Common Press, 1984.

Far Out the Coils. The Tashmoo Press, 1985.

Index

This modest memoir—quiet, affectionate, down to earth—perfectly embodies the offshore New England life and land it celebrates. Henry Beetle Hough's lifelong love affair with Martha's Vineyard will enthrall admirers of sturdy American traits. For the island and the editor whose name became virtually synonymous with it make this saga of stewardship a model for all who inhabit—or yearn for—places made special by durable care, born of past habit and burnished by future promise. Patience, fortitude, persistence through all the seasons here spell out six decades of impassioned commitment. Méras reveals how Hough uniquely served and conserved the island's three-century heritage, long cherished for nothing spectacular, just as an enduringly livable everyday landscape. Martha's Vineyard matters for its spaces and its skies, for its every hedge and hidden bush, strand and pond, each quotidian headland and unpretentious heath. This account of the Vineyard's champion is a small classic.

> **David Lowenthal, author of *George Perkins Marsh: Prophet of Conservation*
> and *The Past Is a Foreign Country*, American professor emeritus of geography
> at University College, London, and sometime Vineyard resident.**

Tenacious, insular, opinionated, a gifted writer and a dedicated conservationist, Henry Hough never stopped fighting to preserve the natural integrity of the tiny portion of this planet to which he was passionately devoted: Martha's Vineyard Island.

When they acquired the *Vineyard Gazette* in 1920, Hough and his wife Betty launched an unceasing effort to protect the island's limited space, fragile ecology, and beauty from large-scale or heavy-handed real estate development. They succeeded in having large tracts of land set aside as natural sanctuaries and also found time to successfully oppose billboards and to curtail zealous public landscaping including the cutting of overarching branches from roadside trees to facilitate the movement of tour buses.

In their unrelenting zeal the Houghs demonstrated what influence a little, bi-weekly newspaper can exert in a small community. . . . No spot on this globe has ever had a more devoted champion.

> **Nelson Bryant, author of *Fresh Air, Bright Water: Adventures in Wood, Field, and Stream;*
> longtime Woods, Field and Stream columnist for the *New York Times*,
> former New Hampshire newspaper editor, and year-round Vineyarder.**

In the chronicles of life on Martha's Vineyard, and in the story of the conservation movement nationwide, Henry Hough played a sustained and singular part, the effects of which are still felt. Wise, gentle, gifted, uncommonly dedicated, he became, like William Allen White, the kind of country editor whose voice carried far. He and his work ought to be much better known and appreciated, and so this first biography, by his friend and fellow journalist Phyllis Méras, is a highly welcome event.

> **David McCullough, Pulitzer Prize–winning author of
> *1776, John Adams,* and *Truman*, and year-round Vineyarder.**

A vivid and compelling portrait of a great journalist, his life and times, as well as the story behind the creation of one of America's finest weekly newspapers.

> **William Styron, Pulitzer Prize–winning author of *The Confessions of Nat Turner*
> and *Sophie's Choice*, and Vineyard seasonal resident.**